STACKING STONES

STORIES OF GOD'S FAITHFULNESS
IN FAR-OFF PLACES

TOM AND JANINE THROSSEL

This book is dedicated to:

Each missionary friend who worked alongside us,
encouraged and prayed for us. You hold a place of deep
respect and honor in our hearts. We truly love you.

The Bolivian people who took us into their country
with open arms. We learned so much from your
graciousness, wisdom, perseverance and love. *Gracias*.

Our faithful team of supporters. Thank you times a million.
We hope we honor your role in this ministry with our words
and lives. We have truly loved being partners with you.

Soli Deo gloria

*"I was held in Your arms,
Carried for a thousand miles to show
Not for a moment did You forsake me."*

*— "Not for a Moment (After All)"
by Meredith Andrews, Mia Fieldes, Jacob Sooter*

AUTHORS' NOTE:

In writing this book, we relied on our own memories, as well as journal and blog entries, e-mails, letters, other people's accounts, sermon notes and recordings, and researchable data. There are no invented or composite characters in this book. These stories are as true as we can present them. Most names have either been changed or retained with permission. We love all of these people, and hope that is reflected by these writings.

All photographs were taken by Tom and Janine Throssel.

Cover design and interior formatting is by Glendon Haddix of Streetlight Graphics. For more information, we recommend looking over his website at www.streetlightgraphics.com.

The original artwork for "Blossom" was painted by Katie Wells, a dear friend and former teammate with us in Bolivia. It is reprinted here in black and white with her permission. See it in brilliant color and request a free copy for yourself at www.janinethrossel. com.

CONTENTS

PREFACE

By Janine

"Y OU KNOW HOW TO EAT yuca?" The wizened woman smirked up at me as I stood in front of her produce booth.

"Yes." I answered confidently as I held the plant roots in my hands and checked the crackly brown skin for flaws and mildew.

The woman laughed out loud to her companions and the passersby who noticed our conversation. "The gringa knows how to eat yuca!"

I'm sure I blushed in response to the giggles from nearby market stalls as I took my vegetables and dignity elsewhere. *Can I eat yuca? Of course I can eat yuca. And sugarcane, chuño, and mocochinchi peaches to boot. Do I know how to eat yuca? We live in Santa Cruz de la Sierra, for crying out loud.*

I flagged down a green-and-white Toyota Corolla taxi for the ride home. I didn't tell the produce vendor that there were plenty of other things I still didn't know. I knew how to cook the yuca root, but not the delicious dish of red-and-yellow *papalisa* roots I liked so much. After nearly a decade of work among the Bolivian people, I still didn't know how to play the pan flute. I couldn't figure out what *k'jaras* were (although signs advertised the specialty pork dish all across town on Friday nights). And I couldn't seem to avoid walking into the low, sharp edges of the outdoor market's shade tarps.

I hadn't been the most-likely candidate to live in a developing country. My own mother marveled at how her daughter — once on

1

the edge of being a hypochondriac and germaphobe—now brushed ants off sandwiches before eating them and carried rocks to fend off mangy, rabid dogs. But things had changed. I had changed. I had learned to make my own tortillas, sleep standing in queues, hide my cash from pickpockets, rattle avocados to test ripeness, walk through the meat market without holding my breath, change a tank of cooking gas, and identify a woman's birthplace from the length of her skirts. I could sing along with dozens of familiar tunes in Spanish. I could even eat a *salteña*—a delicious handheld meat pie—without spilling a drop of steaming broth. My feet were callused from long, dusty walks in sandals. My stories were sometimes hard for others to hear. I wondered at times what place was really my home.

And now, just when I felt like I had gotten the hang of the whole thing, we were leaving.

Our sons were just three and six years old that morning when our airplane streamed through a cobalt sky and touched down onto Viru Viru International Airport's tarmac for the first time. Now they were young men of twelve and fifteen. We had lived through stellar days and hard ones, but—if given a choice—we wouldn't change any of them. We had seen miracles and survived heartbreak. We had dressed up to lead meetings, conferences, seminars, classes, and church services. We had dressed down and shoveled sand, laid bricks, pulled weeds, scrubbed floors, and painted walls. And through all those moments, one thing remained.

God was faithful.

Always.

INTRODUCTION

By Tom

I'M THE SECOND-BORN OF FOUR sons. As kids, my brothers and I enjoyed many adventures together. When we talk about our childhoods now, however, we each have different memories of the "good old days." One brother will remember a certain incident, and it's not until he begins to talk about it that the others start to recall it too. I'm amazed that I need to be reminded of events that once seemed life changing.

I don't think I'm the only one with this problem, though. Everyone forgets from time to time.

The ancient Israelites sure did. They failed to remember the astounding things God did for them, including some of the most visually-stunning miracles of all time. God even delivered them out of slavery in Egypt and led them through the middle of the Red Sea on dry ground. Yet they quickly forgot these wonders and started complaining, whining, and doubting.

The second time God led the Israelites through a large body of water, He introduced a plan to help them remember. He wanted them to mark, for future generations, His faithfulness to them as they entered the Promised Land. So He told them to gather twelve stones from the dry riverbed and pile them up alongside the Jordan River where that latest miracle had occurred.

God said to the Israelites, "In the future, when your descendants ask their parents, 'What do these stones mean?' tell them, 'Israel crossed the Jordan on dry ground.' For the Lord your God dried up the Jordan before you until you had crossed over... He did this so that all the peoples of the earth might know that the hand of the Lord is powerful and so that you might always fear the Lord your God" (Josh. 4:21-24, New International Version).

The stones reminded the people of God's power. They showed that He does what He promises.

In this book, we share some of our personal stacks of stones — markers of God's faithfulness through more than a decade as missionaries to Latin America. Some of the memories are happy; some are tough. There have been stones of peace, when we wrestled with fear. There have been stones of growth, when God rubbed off some of our rough edges. There have been stones of identity, purpose and citizenship when He reminded us of His plans and love for us. In one way or another, each stone — each memory — reminds our family of God's goodness and provision in our lives.

Janine is definitely the writer in our family, and this book would not exist without her. Many of the short pieces between the chapters were taken from blog entries, journals, and letters she wrote while we worked as missionaries overseas.

We have taken turns writing chapters about situations and events in our lives so that others may read and know how great our God is and some of what He did for us while we served Him in Bolivia. Our prayer is that as you read about God's faithfulness to us, you will be encouraged to begin to build your own stone piles, remembering God's faithfulness in your life as well.

CHAPTER ONE

Provision: Building Up My Rock Pile

By Tom

O NE OF MY STONE PILES is much bigger than the others. Ironically, it represents the part of my life where I tend to struggle the most—trusting God to meet financial needs. Even as I worry about money, our merciful God keeps providing, and every example of His faithfulness gives me another stone for the pile. I visit this monument quite often, especially when I need to remember God's provision for me.

My parents raised my three brothers and me with a strong work ethic. As an adult, I was prepared to take care of my family myself. It didn't work that way when we got to Bolivia, however. We were "faith missionaries" there, which means we didn't have a set dollar amount coming in from an employer each month. Instead, we raised pledges from individuals and churches who, in turn, gave toward a monthly target amount that covered our housing, food, and other expenses. If we were short on finances, I couldn't just put in more hours or take a second position. I had to wait, pray, and be faithful to do my job. If people didn't follow through on their pledges and send money, there would be less for us to withdraw.

Such utter reliance on God and other people was a huge challenge for me. In a way, it was a great experience because each check we received—from one dollar to thousands—reminded us that we were loved and cared for, that people believed in us. But the learning curve was steep, and it was hard not to worry.

I could spend all day sharing how God took care of us in Bolivia. But the story of His provision in our lives didn't start when we went to South America. Long before we stepped on foreign soil, He was already preparing me to trust.

Janine and I got married in 1993. About a year later, I sold my motorcycle and old Chevy Blazer, she gave up her car, and we prepared to leave Northern California for Moody Bible Institute in Chicago. At Moody, I would begin working toward my bachelor's degree in missionary aviation, which would prepare me to work as a mechanic on small, single-engine airplanes in Bolivia.

We packed up the minivan my father-in-law helped us buy and headed for Illinois. Everything we brought had to fit in that van. Even though it was crammed full from floor to ceiling, we had no bed, no dresser, and no couch. We didn't have much of anything, actually — except each other and a lot of enthusiasm.

Somewhere along the way — Nebraska or Iowa, perhaps — I turned to Janine and said, "Maybe when we get to Chicago, we can buy a bean bag chair."

Sinking into a cushy bean bag after the long, cross-country drive sounded great to me, even though we had no money to buy one. She shrugged politely. "Sure. We'll see."

Many miles and hours later, these two country kids arrived in the big city. After setting aside money to cover our first month's rent and security deposit, plus pay Janine's initial month of school fees, we had ten dollars left.

When we went to the rental agency to pick up the keys to our apartment, we discovered it wouldn't be ready until the next day. After hearing that we had no family nearby and no money for a hotel, the agency representative took pity on us and agreed to give us the keys at four o'clock that afternoon instead.

Our friendly new neighbors saw us pull into the parking lot and came out to help us unload the van. It took about ten minutes.

We expected to live simply at first, at least until I had a job with a steady paycheck. We planned to hang up sheets over the curtain rods and sleep in sleeping bags on our bedroom floor.

But the place didn't even have hooks or rods over the windows. There was no plush rug to sleep on either, just hard tile in the bedroom and a worn-out, filthy carpet in the living room that the landlord promised to replace. This was not what we expected, by any stretch of the imagination.

As we were unpacking our meager inventory of household goods, our new neighbors knocked on the door. A huge, forty-foot moving truck was parked just outside the apartment complex. More people were moving in, and it was our turn to help.

The new couple was as surprised by the small size of their apartment as we were with the condition of ours. They quickly realized all their furniture wasn't going to fit, and after unloading a few items, the husband, Jim, asked if we could use their extra bed.

Can we use a bed? Bring it on in!

As we helped Jim and his wife unload the truck, their apartment became so full that we couldn't walk through it. So they started moving more stuff into *our* apartment. They didn't want to be paid for anything; they just wanted to give it to us. We didn't know them — we had barely spoken to them. Yet they were filling our apartment with exactly what we needed. When the truck was empty, we closed our door behind us and just stood there, amazed at God's care for us.

A few minutes later, there was another knock at the door. It was Jim, holding something out towards me.

"My wife won't let me keep it; we don't have room," he said. "Do you want my bean bag chair?"

Only Janine and God knew what I had said when we were driving down that long stretch of freeway. We marveled at how He was providing — not just for our needs, but for relatively minor wants like a comfy bean bag chair.

And we didn't have to sleep one night on that cold, hard tile floor.

We spent three years at Moody's Biblical Studies program in Chicago, then transferred to the school's Missionary Aviation Technology program in Tennessee. Unknown to us, the curriculum there was so intense that students weren't allowed to work while attending school. Janine had to find a job, but we were newcomers in a small town and people were hesitant to hire her at first. When she finally found a position, our older son, Peter, was only about a year old.

Thanks to generous donors, Moody students in Chicago did not pay any tuition. Aviation training is expensive, however. My cost for the program in Tennessee was $1,000 a month. Janine was working hard, and with the financial support of a few family members and friends, we managed to pay our living expenses. The school bill was too much.

Financial aid typically went to senior students closer to graduation. School officials assured us that God would provide, but Janine and I were doubtful. If nothing changed, we could be more than $20,000 in debt by the time I was done and never get to South America. After prayerful consideration, we concluded that this scenario wouldn't work, and I told my class supervisor I had to quit.

He wouldn't hear of it. Instead, he suggested we write to friends and family at home and ask them to finance my remaining education.

We spent about fifty dollars we didn't have on stamps, envelopes, and photocopies, and sent out the letter. After three weeks, Janine said, "You have to quit school. We can't afford this."

But we had already completed three years in Chicago, jumped through all the hoops of getting into the aviation program, and moved to Tennessee. I really didn't want to quit. I talked her into waiting one more week, and one person finally responded — with fifty dollars.

But my class supervisor *still* wouldn't let me quit, and neither would the school's director. Rather than accept my resignation from the program, he asked me to come back the next day, this time with Janine.

When we returned to his office, he looked at us squarely. "What would you say if I told you that I contacted a friend of mine here in town, and he's willing to give you a scholarship for a year?" he asked. "Would you stay?"

We stayed.

Before we went to college, we believed we were supposed to join Moody's Missionary Aviation Technology program, and we knew we needed to go to Bolivia. We had stepped forward in faith, not sure how any of this would happen or what roads we would take to get there. We expected it to happen differently, but God provided for us.

And every time He did, it was another stone for the pile.

When it came time to leave Tennessee after I graduated, Pete was three years old and our younger son Philip was nearly three months old. We were headed west this time, to see family and raise financial support before leaving the country. We wanted to reach California in time for the upcoming Thanksgiving holiday.

We had transitioned from the minivan to a Jeep Wagoneer and, by now, had more belongings than would have fit in either one. We rented the biggest U-Haul trailer available, hooked it to the back of the Jeep, and packed it up. Even then, the top of the Jeep was piled high with our kids' toy box and bicycles. We looked a little like the Beverly Hillbillies.

We stayed with family and friends along the way, and were so grateful for all their hospitality. At every stop, we carried in a suitcase for each of us — four or five bags. Hauling all that luggage in and out so often got old very quickly. So we decided to pack a week's worth of clothes for all of us into one suitcase and leave the rest in the truck and trailer.

Near the end of our trip, we planned to stay one night in Phoenix before traveling on to Twentynine Palms, California, the next day. Over a wonderful meal, Janine's relatives tried to talk us into staying for Thanksgiving, but I kept insisting, "We have to get the trailer back — it's a rental."

The next morning, I got up early, opened the garage door, and walked out onto the street with our one shared suitcase. Much to my dismay, the Jeep was gone, along with the rented trailer and everything that was in it! I wondered at first if it was a joke, Janine's family trying to extend our visit. But it wasn't a joke. Our Jeep, trailer and possessions were gone.

9

When the officer who answered the phone at the police department heard my story, his first comment was short and to the point: "Welcome to Phoenix, Car Theft Capital of the U.S."[1]

Hurt and angry, I began to think about all the irreplaceable things that were gone— my grandfather's coin collection, the stamps my mom had collected with my great-grandfather. Who would do such a thing? How? Why?

We didn't have much. The trailer was full of theology books, inexpensive clothes, kids' toys, and secondhand furniture—none of it worth much money. But it was ours.When I went inside, our three-year-old son was sitting at a table, singing a song from an old Disney video about Johnny Appleseed. I stopped to listen.

> The Lord is good to me
> and so I thank the Lord
> for giving me the things I need:
> the sun, and the rain,
> and the apple seed.
> The Lord is good to me![2]

I began to cry, not because of what we had lost, but because I realized that my preschooler understood what I didn't—that God was good no matter what we had or how hard times were. We had one suitcase of belongings and a diaper bag—and everything we needed.

My young family was blessed. God was still good. He is always enough.

I was still hurt, though, because I wasn't sure what He was doing with us. I called my Aunt Joyce—a pillar in my life—and told her what had happened.

"Oh, Tommy," she said. "I'm so excited!"

I thought she had heard me wrong, so I repeated the story.

---

1 Sure enough, Phoenix would own that label shortly after our robbery. After that, the unfavorable title moved on to other cities, most of them in California where we lived!

2 Lyrics from "The Lord is Good to Me," from Walt Disney's *Melody Time*. Words and music by Kim Gannon and Walter Kent. © 1946 Walt Disney Music Co. Copyright renewed. All rights reserved. Used by permission.

"I heard what you said exactly," she told me. "I'm just excited to see what God's going to do!"

As it turned out, Aunt Joyce's faith in God showed me again that he had bigger plans than I did.

Because we no longer had a vehicle, we rented a car, and continued our journey. Janine's family in Arizona generously provided us with bedding and extra clothes, as well as books and toys for our sons. In Southern California, we stayed with friends who filled the car with more gifts and gave us a check from someone we had never met. Again, our God was providing for us through these compassionate people.

When we finally made it back to my parents' house in Northern California, we were exhausted and just wanted to rest. They had set up a guest room for us and graciously agreed to let us stay with them until we figured out our next step.

From the moment we arrived, we were overwhelmed by the generosity of others. The guest room was outfitted with a new bed, a dresser, and more books and clothes — all for us. Friends from Tennessee who heard what happened had sent handmade quilts, along with our favorite tea and barbecue sauce. Family members gave us furniture and other household items. As time went on, we received a refrigerator, microwave, barbecue grill, kitchen table, and chairs. When we finally were able to rent a place of our own, it was furnished entirely with gifts.

During that time, we weren't simply blessed by God's outpouring of provision, but also by the *way* that He gave to us. We would have appreciated any kind of furniture, any style of clothes. But He showed His love in a very personal way.

Years before our kids were born, Janine dreamed of owning a Jenny Lind crib with a cherry finish. But when we were expecting our first son, we couldn't afford to be choosy.

One afternoon, our minivan overheated as Janine was driving home from college in Chicago. She pulled over to let the car cool off. A nearby house was having a garage sale, and when she went over to have a look around, she found the very crib she had always wanted — same style, color and brand — for only $20!

Peter and, later, Philip slept in that crib — until it was stolen in

11

the robbery. But when we got to California, we were amazed to find one exactly like it waiting for us in my parents' guest room — complements of the local crisis pregnancy center.

This sort of thing kept happening. We often found ourselves laughing because people who didn't know us, had never seen our home in Tennessee, and didn't know our personal preferences brought us items that were exact replicas of some of our favorite things that had been stolen. Janine received an unusually styled dress that looked just like one she had taken from her in Arizona. One of Peter's favorite books — a rare volume that most people had never heard of — was replaced. An antique knickknack someone gave us to use as a decoration in our new house had Janine's maiden name written on it in small print — and the giver didn't even know her maiden name.

God provided far more than we could have dreamed possible, but He wasn't done yet.

During aviation maintenance school, I took out an $8,000 loan to pay for the required aviation toolkit (it's hard to be a mechanic without good tools). I had repaid only half the loan when we were robbed. In California, I was offered a job at a small airport where I could gain experience and pay bills while raising funds to go to Bolivia. There was only one problem. The employer offered the job on the condition that I brought my own equipment. I had the debt, but not the tools.

We had been invited to speak at my parents' church the Sunday after we arrived in California. I planned to talk about our upcoming move and the work that I hoped to do with the aviation team in South America. I planned to tell them how SAMAIR Bolivia — the missions organization we were working with — used airplanes as lifesaving tools. They fly pastors, doctors, and missionaries out to remote villages and give ill and injured people flights back to the main city for treatment.

But as we dressed for the service in our hand-me-down clothes, we felt a little awkward. I told Pastor Dale that I didn't want to tell everyone the sad story about the robbery because I felt like a charity case.

"You know what charity is, don't you?" he asked. "It's love. Let them love on you."

After we spoke about our future work, the pastor explained how we had been robbed just days before and asked the congregation to take up a collection for us.

That small church raised $4,000 for us in one morning.

Janine and I were touched by the "charity" they had shown us. In private, we considered our options. Should we pay off the loan and start fresh from there? Should we invest that $4,000 in a second set of tools and risk being caught in debt that might delay our departure? Should we do something else with it? What was the wisest decision?

Late that night, I got a call from a stranger who had attended church that day. Turns out, he had attended aviation school but later decided to return to carpentry. He still had his aviation tools, he said, and he wanted to give them to us.

At first, I thought he was joking, or that maybe he had a small, handheld toolbox with a few cheap tools in it. But his toolkit was even more expensive than mine had been. These were brand-new, top-of-the-line tools in a shiny red box. I offered to give him the $4,000 from the church, but he wouldn't take it.

"The Lord told me to give them to you," he said humbly. "It would be disobedient if I took a penny for them." We ended up using the church's offering to repay our debt for the first set.

The new toolbox was so heavy that it nearly bottomed out my dad's small pickup truck when we loaded it up. I used those tools for nearly two years in California and then brought them with us to South America where they were used to maintain the mission's planes.

For years afterwards, people would ask, "Where did you get such nice tools?" Over and over, I got to share this unbelievable story.

And there was one more surprise. The theft of our photo albums was hard on my wife. Family members kindly sent a few replacement copies of pictures from our wedding day, and those were precious gifts. But the rest of our wedding photos, as well as scores of baby and birthday photos, were gone. I was hopeful that the police might recover my tools in a pawn shop somewhere (they never did), but neither of us expected to see those photos again.

Aunt Joyce's daughter, Star, and Janine's sister, Andrea, had more faith than that. They boldly told Janine they were praying for the return of our wedding pictures.

Several weeks later, the U-Haul trailer was recovered. The rental company sent us a cardboard box of the things they found on the floor, including a single shoe and a piece of a toy. But that's not all. The box also contained a stack of yearbooks, a manila envelope with a set of proofs and negatives from our wedding, and a cracked, chipped plastic container holding almost every photo negative from the birth of our first child to the birth of our second — three years' worth of remembrances.

That Christmas, a local church and some of Janine's family members gave us money to reprint those negatives. Janine's mom gave us new baby books so we could rewrite memories. We had full photo albums again.

God didn't have to orchestrate the return of those precious mementos, but He did it anyway. We eventually saw that this trial wasn't designed to keep us from our dream in Bolivia, but to strengthen us for it.

Now, when I worry about our future, when our finances get tight, and when I wonder how I'm going to pay a bill, I go back to this pile of stones we collected before we ever left the country. I remember Chicago and the bean bag chair. I remember Phoenix. I remember the tools. I remember when God provided.

He is faithful.

Even when I doubt.

Shortly before we finished language school and moved to Bolivia, we enjoyed a day with our sons at a Costa Rican wildlife park.

TRANSITION

By Janine

I N LANGUAGE SCHOOL, TOM AND I *were told that culture shock could attack us like a thousand nicks, one seemingly small wound at a time, invasively and cumulatively, until we succumbed to it like the* Chinese torture of lingchi.

Well, that didn't sound very appealing.

We were determined to stand strong against such an adversary. By the time we left Costa Rica, our first Latin home, we were used to walking long distances, taking public transportation, surviving hot weather, eating unusual food, and looking for products in the market that didn't bear the usual brand marks we recognized from the United States. We were confident we could handle it.

But when we arrived in Bolivia, we still had so much to learn. We needed to know the different Bolivian greetings for men and women and the key phrases that would get us better prices at the markets. We needed to adapt to the smell of raw meat hanging in the open air and the vendors selling cow's-foot jelly on the street. I had to learn to offer something to drink as soon as a guest walked through my door. I had to learn to serve food on a tray and not just hand my friends a bag of chips or a glass of soda.

I had begun to understand the relaxed drawl of Mexican Spanish and the clipped, formal speech of my Costa Rican instructors. But I had to learn the accent of Santa Cruz, Bolivia, too. Words there were often formed without the letter "s," which led to some misunderstandings. Despues sounded like "deh-PWAY." Mas o menos sounded like "mah-

16

oh-may-no." Sometimes, it felt like we were starting over with learning Spanish, or el castellano. They didn't even call it español!

From shopping to cooking to walking our dogs, we didn't seem to fit sometimes. We raised eyebrows and prompted laughter and comments. We got homesick. We got tired. We got lonely and frustrated. Housework in this new place – without dishwashers, vacuum cleaners, or hot running water – was a struggle. I felt guilty for plopping my children in front of Spanish cartoons while I tried to keep up with it all.

But we pressed onward. We refused to give up. Those thousand nicks were not going to do us in.

We arrived in Bolivia in March 2003. By the following October, we already had endured several funerals, sicknesses, and transitions. There had been blockades in the country as the Bolivian gas war came to a head. The president was being thrown out of the palace. I had heard, read, and seen enough vigilante beatings and lynchings in the news to make my stomach turn.

And there was something else. In the midst of all this, our six-week-old niece, Elizabeth Grace, died in the United States. We never got to meet her, except through photos and e-mails.

Tom's parents came to visit us right after the memorial service held in little Elizabeth's honor. They, too, were tired in body and soul. They, too, had suffered many nicks of their own that year.

Together, we traveled to the mountains. We stood beneath waterfalls that washed away the noise and dust of the city. We rumbled over gravel roads and climbed higher and higher – toward the sky and away from the stresses we left behind. We built a campfire and looked up at the stars.

We climbed to a place called Samaipata – a Quechua word that means "resting in the heights." Not far away is an old fort called El Fuerte, or "the Strong One." As I looked out across the green mountaintops, the wind blowing almost silently, I felt the calm comfort of rest.

I breathed in fresh air while deep peace engulfed me. I thought of the Strong One who had brought us to this place, and of the Bible verses that say, "I lift up my eyes to the hills. From where does my help come? My help comes from the Lord, who made heaven and earth" (Ps. 121:1-2, English Standard Version).

I realized that, if we were to cope with the culture shock of the valley

17

below and fulfill all that was in store for us in this new land, I didn't need to be tougher and fight better. It sounded counterintuitive, but we didn't need to work harder. We needed to rest more completely – in God's strength, on the heights of His love. We needed to give out of the overflow that He would keep giving to us.

We could accomplish some great things in the name of charity. We could feed the hungry, clothe the needy, build buildings, and implement programs. But we couldn't give people the lasting, unconditional love they needed for their souls. Only God could do that. As the apostle Paul wrote to the people of Corinth centuries ago, if we did a lot of amazing things without love, we would be nothing and gain nothing.

A few months later, my husband, sons, and I returned to those same hills for a conference and retreat. There, a musical group from the States sang a rich hymn from the late 1800s, penned by an Irish woman named Jean Sophia Pigott.

Jesus! I am resting, resting in the joy of what Thou art;

I am finding out the greatness of Thy loving heart...

Yes, I rest in Thee, Beloved, know what wealth of grace is Thine,

Know Thy certainty of promise, and have made it mine.

Simply trusting Thee, Lord Jesus, I behold Thee as Thou art, And Thy love, so pure, so changeless, satisfies my heart; Satisfies its deepest longings, meets, supplies its every need, Compasseth me round with blessings: Thine is love indeed!

Ever lift Thy face upon me as I work and wait for Thee; Resting 'neath Thy smile, Lord Jesus, Earth's dark shadows flee.[3]

---

3 Pigott, Jean S. "Jesus, I Am Resting, Resting." Lyrics published in 1876. Copyright: Public Domain.

We would need to rest through more funerals, homesickness, tiredness, and culture shock. We would need to find rest when our kids faced bullies, when the house flooded, when we dealt with heavy workloads, and when people we loved came and then went. We would need to rest when things didn't go our way, and rest in celebration when they did.

But when we rested, God's grace abounded. In those early days, He was already allowing us to pile up rocks of remembrance.

Like the sheltering, pink-petaled branches of the Tajibo and Toborochi trees, our God would be beauty, refuge, shade, and glory over us. He is the One who would heal each of our thousand nicks, day after day, before they had a chance to fester. He is the One who gave us strength and love from His unending supply.

After years of learning and leaning on Him, I have found that His love – so pure and so changeless – still satisfies my heart.

CHAPTER TWO

IDENTITY: WHO AM I?

By Janine

SUNSHINE STREAMED THROUGH THE CLASSROOM windows as I sat nervously before the *profe*. She smiled at me, but it was hard to smile back.

I had prepared diligently for this oral exam, but I hadn't seen this question coming. Name? Yes. Age? Fine. Family members? Sure. I could answer all those inquiries in Spanish with ease. I had rehearsed with friends and was ready to explain why I was there, what my future plans were, and what my life had been like in the United States. I was eager for the grade that would usher me into my next quarter of language school classes. But her question left me stunned.

"What is hardest for you about being here in Costa Rica?" she asked.

Thoughts surged through my brain so quickly it brought physical pain. *I miss my family. The furniture is hard. The walk to school is long. I get sick so easily.* It hurt even to think of the "thousand nicks" that we ignored daily to learn someone else's culture and language.

Then I had a moment of clarity, of sudden calm. I knew the answer.

"No one understands me."

I didn't mean that my words were often misunderstood. Yes, I once used a phrase incorrectly over and over again in a classroom speech. Another time someone thought I was saying *hormigas* (Spanish for ants) when I was intending to talk about *origami* — the Asian art of folding paper. And I sometimes chose the "number two for English" option instead of ordering my pizzas in Spanish.

I had expected the language barrier. But what hurt more than the hard furniture was that no one seemed to understand me — my heart and my intentions.

After Tom and I announced that we were going to work as missionaries in Latin America, North Americans tended to put me in one of two camps: I was a saint, or I was stupid.

Those who thought we were candidates for sainthood said things like, "You're such a wonderful person. I could never do that." I wondered if they thought I was somehow immune from the pain of moving abroad, of leaving my country and family behind.

I wasn't.

Those who put me in the stupid camp said things like, "You know we could find you a job in the States — you have marketable skills." Believe me; I had thoroughly considered a steady paycheck and an office with a view.

Some of the Latins, on the other hand, put me in a third camp — suspicious. This would be the case especially after we left language school, when I was settling into my new host country in South America.

In light of world history, one could hardly blame them for their doubts about foreigners. Documents like the *Dum Diversas* from 1452 or the *Requerimiento* of 1513 proclaimed that God had given Europeans the right to subjugate, war against, enslave, and even kill natives if they did not do as they were instructed. The chilling threats, gross arrogance, and horrible insanity of those papers still invoke shudders today. Even centuries later, North Americans continue to come into their country bullying, bossing, and bribing to get their way.

Yet we perpetrated none of that. I didn't consider myself superior to the Bolivian people. I struggled with some of the prejudiced opinions that were leveled at me because of things done in years past by and to people I had never known.

I remember one difficult day in particular. A taxi driver dropped me off in front of the small house Tom and I were renting. It was the place where the floor was thick with dead cockroaches the night we moved in. It was the one with no shade in our sons' tiled play yard. It was the one with the tiny bathroom where I had to do contortions to fill a plastic bucket under the electrically charged showerhead for my preschooler's baths.

I was in a taxi that day because we had given up our family's vehicles to come to Bolivia. I didn't even have a valid driver's license in this foreign country. Don't get me wrong—I did it readily. I did it out of love for this nation of people that I had yet to know and fully understand. I was willing to give up my extended family, home, career, possessions, and even some rights and freedom to try to make a difference in the poorest nation in South America.

People didn't understand. Instead, they asked why we would proselytize people who were perfectly fine without our help. We weren't proselytizing, and Bolivian nationals repeatedly asked for our help. We forced no one to change religions, to accept either us or our God. We submitted to their laws, learned their language, and respected our position as guests in their country. We listened and lived with them. We spoke honestly to them. We offered what we could to heal their bodies, homes, families, and souls. But there were no strings attached — ever. We had been given much in our own lives, so we gave out of gratitude.

It was love.

I didn't explain all this to the taxi driver that day. I said very little except for polite formalities and chit-chat. Yet, he railed at me as he came down my street. "You came to this country to live like a king off the backs of the Bolivian people!"

A king? Seriously?

I looked at our little single-story house. It had three rosebushes in the yard, a neatly painted concrete wall to keep out intruders, and French doors in the kitchen to let sunshine in on one side. It was a pretty house, and we were blessed to live there.

But the taxi driver couldn't see what I left behind. Most of all, he didn't know how I missed my family and how my heart ached for them every single day. A mansion with a pool and a Lamborghini in the garage wouldn't have made up for that.

We hadn't come to live off the backs of the Bolivian people. In fact, the reverse was true. I was offering them my own back, to labor among them. I wasn't a saint as some suggested, but I wasn't their enemy, either.

Nadie me comprende. No one understands me.

Late in my first year in Bolivia, I was introduced to a group of girls who would change me forever. Those girls knew what it meant to be misunderstood.

I met them in an orphanage, but very few actually were orphans. Most had been abused, and all of them had been abandoned or relinquished to the government's care. Many of them likely would have said along with me, "*Nadie me comprende.* No one understands me."

When I met them, most were in elementary school or junior high. As I watched them grow, my concern grew. For some insensible reason, the sins of their parents were charged to them. Some of the parents had been abusive and neglectful, but it was the girls who were scorned and belittled. Though they were working to get a good education, learn job skills, and be respectable ladies, people made comments to them that suggested their future was sealed by their past.

I didn't believe that. Their biological families may have failed them, but their heavenly Father was the Almighty. He could do whatever He wanted with their lives, couldn't He?

But oh, how people talk. I heard chatter around them, talking the girls down and pushing them toward the cultural norm of teen pregnancy and early marriage.

Getting pregnant wouldn't automatically turn their boyfriends into husbands, or even keep those men close by. It wouldn't build the families and self-worth they wanted. It had the potential to perpetuate the unhealthy brokenness in which their lives had begun. But it seemed that motherhood was the best that society expected of these young women. That, and nothing else.

I didn't want these precious girls to have that mindset — that their value would be determined by their attractiveness, marriages, or number of children. It's a wonderful thing to be a wife and mother, but many of these young women misconstrued the purpose of those roles. Being a mom wouldn't validate them or create their worth. They didn't see that they were all priceless — with children or without them.

Many people helped these girls in various ways, providing food, clothing, shelter, and education. But for a season, as leaders came and went, they lacked solid teaching about their identity — who they were and how valuable they were. That burdened my heart.

While in the United States for several months, I felt a stirring inside to create something for these girls and others like them. With the help of family, US friends, and coworkers, we developed what would become our initial series of "Princess Conferences" for girls ages eight through twelve. We prayed for eighty girls to come that first weekend — forty on each of two days. When 120 girls throughout the city signed up to attend, we were thrilled to schedule a third day.

The conference schedule included games, music, a meal, and a poignant drama production based on Beth Moore's book for children, *A Parable about the King*.[4] But the lessons we shared during class times were the part we most wanted the girls to catch.

We taught these young ladies that they are children of God, and that daughters of the King of Kings are princesses. We told them that, just as princesses are beautiful, God has instilled beauty

---

4 Published by B&H Kids, 2003. The 2007 edition was titled, *My Child, My Princess: A Parable About the King*.

in each of them. We explained that princesses are supposed to be kind and well-spoken, that they work to make the world a better place. Likewise, we encouraged each young lady in attendance to be kind and well-spoken, and to do her part to improve her world. And just as princesses have a royal lineage, so could they—no matter their background—as part of the royal family of Christ.

I didn't want the girls just to come, listen to speeches and songs, and leave. I wanted each one to be able to ask questions or express concerns to someone. So each table of about seven girls had a "counselor" with them throughout the day. Some of these counselors were North Americans, while many others were Bolivian nationals. Not only were the nationals able to speak easily with the girls in their own language, they also understood their culture better than we did. We were very grateful for their presence.

One of my favorite memories from the weekend of conferences was when the group from the orphanage came.

We didn't let all the orphanage girls sit together. We separated them into groups of two or three and seated them at different tables. We hoped doing this would allow them to get to know some of the other children.

As part of the section on beauty, the girls played a game that involved putting makeup on one person at each table. Some of the groups got wild and crazy with their cosmetics, leaving their "model" looking like a pastel-toned circus clown. But others took time to apply the makeup very carefully.

As I walked from table to table, a Bolivian group leader called me over to look at the contestant picked by her team.

"Isn't she pretty?" the leader asked.

I looked at Sofía, one of the girls from the children's home. I had known her for about four years. She wore what she was given—usually very casual outfits of shorts and tank tops or t-shirts and jeans. She went to school when and where she was told. She slept in an assigned girls' dorm room, on a twin-size bunk bed with no pillow until my mother-in-law made her one.

This day, she forced her eyes to meet mine, looking as if she were hoping for a kind word but not necessarily expecting one. When I told her she looked fabulous, she denied it, dropping her head.

"Yes, you do, Sofía!" I emphatically replied.

"No, not me," she answered again.

The leader of the table and some of the other girls tried to help me persuade her, but she refused to admit either her physical transformation with the makeup or the beauty inherent in her since her creation. She wasn't the only one, either. After years of hearing the lies, these girls now battled a double-edged sword. They didn't just fight what society thought of them — they fought what they thought of themselves.

In a sense, I get that. As a girl, I wasn't a big fan of my freckles, glasses, and skinny legs. But although I worried far too long about what people thought of me, deep down, I knew that other people didn't define my worth. I was blessed to have other voices encouraging me. For every smart-aleck bully who teased me about my pale skin or strawberry-blonde locks, there was a friend, neighbor, relative or church member telling me my complexion was lovely or that they wished they had hair the color of mine. I was told I was smart, talented, well-behaved, and good. Beyond that, I was told that I was a child of God, and the only opinion that really mattered was His. That positive input made it so much easier to shake off the negative attention of the few. I could easily imagine my heavenly Father calling me "Daughter I love" because I heard it from my earthly daddy.

These girls didn't have parents calling them names like sweetheart or beloved. Some of their neighbors didn't want them around. Their relatives had abandoned them. Who would tell them the only opinion that mattered was that of the God who created and loved them as daughters?

The lesson that I was privileged to present at the conference that weekend was about royal lineage and family lines. As I spoke that day, I thought specifically of the orphanage girls who were scattered throughout the room. I talked about the failings of parents. I told them how God never fails, but instead has said, "Can a woman forget her nursing child, that she should have no compassion on the son of her womb? Even these may forget, yet I will not forget you" (Isa. 49:15 ESV). We talked about God's desire to adopt them into His family, make them His daughters, and have them understand that fully.

I cared about every single girl in attendance. Yet these few who came from such hard places were the ones I spoke to most earnestly, because I knew part of their story.

I was moved deeply to see that our labors weren't in vain as girls' hearts and thoughts were changed that day. They prayed with us and talked with us and each other about this idea that God could love them just as they are.

One girl stood in the middle of the classroom, awestruck at the sight before her. My team had transformed the space with decorative balloons and tables spread with linen, china, and "special-occasion" food. Ushers escorted the girls down a red carpet walkway to their seats. "You did all this—for me?" the stunned girl asked. We loved telling her that she was worth it.

I always like to give away some kind of memento when I teach conferences or classes like these. I didn't want the girls to come just for free gifts, but I did want to provide a little something to remind them of what they heard.

For this conference, volunteers made crowns of ribbons and fabric roses to adorn the girls' heads and remind them that they are princesses, daughters of the King. After the conference was over, we were passing through a neighborhood in a different part of town and saw girls wearing their crowns as they played in the street. I visited a little girl who lived in squalor in another neighborhood, and her delicate headdress was hanging up on a drab, smelly wall.

They remembered. They were valued and loved.

I believe that when we truly know who we are—from the girl in the orphanage to the woman on stage teaching her—it changes how we live. When we are not living for the applause and approval of other people, we can embrace our goals and passions fearlessly. When we know that our worth is not conditional on our looks, behavior, background, or the opinions of others, then we can rest. We can stop trying to be "perfect enough" and get on with living to our full capacity. We can stop hiding behind masks that waste our time and energy, and instead be everything that we were made to be.

It's true for each of those girls. It's also true for me, whether I'm in my own country blending in with those around me, or overseas and as different from my neighbors as I could be. We are our best when we are living in the fullness of who He created us to be.

We are God's children.

I am God's child.

And whether anyone else understands me or not, He truly does.

Janine was all smiles during a moment of rest on the first day of Princess Conferences. If you look closely, you might be able to see a row of roses on her head – part of her princess crown.

BLOSSOM

By Janine

I N BOLIVIA, A TALL TREE *grows in a poor place, covered with flowers that change from lemon to scarlet as they bloom and die in a single day. Metaphorically, it is linked with children I love. Sometimes, I want to change their circumstances, to take them back to America with me. Yet most are right where they need to be, growing mighty through the struggle.*

Blossom

A rarity, anomaly

stop still

eyes caught

in a dark world

a bright spot

Muddy rivers flow down

they rush and flee to who-knows-where

Rivers of dishwater

from the kitchen-bedroom-sala

Rivers from an outhouse

that doubles as a shower

Rivers of rain

from a heavy tropic sky

Rivers of pain
from a dying child's eyes
Flow down, down
out and away from here
fleeing, rushing who-knows-where
but out of here

Massive
The mighty tree stands, commands
in muck
eyes to sky
in filth and yet
branches high
reaching, spreading up and out
across the space and mess and pain
Arms of wood
so strong, wide, imposing
Arms of leaves
that shelter, shade, all-knowing
Arms of flowers
their bright lights glowing
Arms of hope
in spite of all, growing
Stretch up and out
to touch beyond what's here
sweep and lean towards the fences
extend from here

Transplant
Of lifting it and shifting it
I dream
pulling roots
tough old wood with
fresh new shoots
A tree so strong should be viewed
admired somewhere far from here
It should grow in cleaner streets
in a pristine park
Cleanliness of hands
reach to touch the bark
Clean wide trails
lead to a copper plaque
Clean split rails
hold curious youngsters back
Couldn't a tree branch out more
if not tethered here?
Be better, stronger, sweeter elsewhere
so far from here?

Petals
Fine design in gentle lines
yellow skin
peach blush
Master Artist's
divine brush
Loose blossoms drifting down

they drop so soft on mud right here
I'm astonished by thick leaves
turned green with brutal heat
Astonished — hues grow richer
when flowers fall like wheat
Astonished — sticky muck
keeps thirsty roots from panting
Astonished by the miracle
that blooms, submissive to the planting
Drift down, down
never carried out from here
thriving, growing Who-knows-how
but here, right here

Blossom, painted by Katie Wells, 2015. You can see this lovely work of art in color, or even get your own copy, at www.janinethrossel.com.

CHAPTER THREE

MIRACLES: MORE THAN I EXPECTED

By Janine

I ONCE READ ABOUT A MAN who offered a million dollars to the first person who could prove to him that a documentable, legitimate miracle had occurred. But because he started from the premise that supernatural miracles were nonexistent, when he was presented with evidence, he tried hard to refute it. X-rays could be faked, right? Witnesses could lie. He asked for miracles that were created before his eyes and under his prearranged conditions. In short, he was asking for an occurrence that could not be proven by science, yet was proven scientifically to be a miracle. Talk about flawed logic!

I felt sorry for this man. For one thing, he had a terribly incorrect view of both the supernatural and of science. After all, if someone insists the sky is green, resists all evidence to the contrary, and renames it on his own say-so, how will he ever see it as the brilliant blue it is? Secondly, the man seemed to be more focused on the miracle itself than on whatever or whomever may have created it. Isn't that all too common these days — to worry and wonder about signs from heaven and yet completely ignore the bigger God who might be sending them?

I don't need a million dollars, but my life has been filled with miracles. I could write an entire book about those experiences alone. One particular miracle that we witnessed in Bolivia especially rocked our world and transformed some of my thoughts about God in the twenty-first-century Americas.

I don't remember much about the phone call — I think that it might have been from our pastor. I don't remember much about the taxi ride that I must have taken. I do remember praying — possibly harder than I had prayed for anything in my whole life: "Please don't let him die!"

Daniel was a friend of my children, the same age as Philip. He also was in my Sunday school class, which probably is why they called me to come when tragedy struck. How could a five-year-old be so healthy and full of life one minute and struggling so hard to survive the next?

I remember racing up the steps of an unfamiliar hospital, noting the gray walls, gray steps, and dirty corners. I remember the framed poster that hung on one wall, a photo of a Caucasian nurse with her fingers to her lips, saying, "Shh." Dressed in a pristine white cap and smock, the woman must have posed for that shot before I was born.

I topped a flight or two of stairs, my heart beating wildly. "Please, God, don't let him die!" I prayed.

But I was too late. Death had beaten me to him.

It was a holiday, *Dia de los Muertos* or "Day of the Dead," when people paid homage to deceased loved ones. At cemeteries, graves were adorned with beer, decorative bread, and cigarettes. Flowers — real and artificial — were everywhere. Inside homes, individuals built little shrines — wooden steps laden with offerings and covered in black cloth.

Because of the festivities, Daniel didn't have to go to school that day, and his parents didn't have to go to work. At a family gathering, Daniel began to play a game of ball. When he followed the rolling ball out into the street, a car struck him dead on.

His abdomen was hit first and some of his organs were decimated. Then he ricocheted to the side of the road on his head. Brain trauma added to little Daniel's internal injuries.

His mother, Ana, met me outside his room because they wouldn't even let her in to see him. But she didn't need to be admitted; she prayed where she sat.

And God heard her there.

"All through this city today," she told me in Spanish, "people are breathing death. I prayed life for my son."

And God answered.

Daniel started moaning. He was alive and asking for his mama.

I, the missionary, marveled at her faith. Who does that? Who prays for the dead to live again?

Some people insist that God doesn't do miracles on this earth anymore. I believe He does because I've seen so many. I've seen rainstorms started and stopped with prayer. I've seen people healed of tremendously scary things.

But death to life? That was a stretch, even for me.

In the biblical story of Lazarus as told in the eleventh chapter of Mark, Jesus gets word that His friend Lazarus is sick. He's dying, in fact. But Jesus didn't respond quite like I did when I got word about Daniel's accident. Jesus didn't run fast, crying for mercy. He stayed where he was for two more days. Why? Because He knew the future. He actually said, "This sickness is not to end in death, but for the glory of God, so that the Son of God may be glorified by it" (John 11:4, New American Standard Bible). Notice He said that the illness wouldn't *end* in death, not that His friend wouldn't pass through death.

Jesus loved this family, which was made up of Lazarus and his sisters, Mary and Martha. The Bible says that love is the very reason He didn't rush to meet them. Because of His love for them, He had a bigger thing to show them than simply healing Lazarus from his illness. They couldn't yet see that there were other factors in play.

Jesus' disciples — the men who were with him — didn't know what was coming either. They weren't thinking of death and life when Jesus said, "Our friend Lazarus has fallen asleep; but I go, so that I may awaken him out of sleep."

No, they were thinking in literal terms. They answered, "Lord, if he has fallen asleep, he will recover."

So Jesus rephrased it — this time with no euphemisms or couched terms.

"Lazarus is dead," He said.

He hadn't gone to where the family was yet, but He already knew.

By the time Jesus finally arrived at His friends' hometown, Lazarus had been in the tomb for four whole days. But get this: Martha knew what God could do. She was like my friend, Ana. Martha said to Jesus, "Lord, if You had been here, my brother would not have died. Even now I know that whatever You ask of God, God will give You."

Even now.

Jesus said to her, "Your brother will rise again."

Martha kind of tested the waters. She had faith enough, but it seems she wanted some clarification. She said, "I know that he will rise again in the resurrection on the last day."

Perhaps she was thinking something like: *Do you mean someday he will rise to life, en route to heaven? Are you speaking of that, Jesus?*

But Jesus said, "I am the resurrection and the life." Jesus held all that power. He could raise Lazarus to life on Judgment Day, or He could raise him at that moment.

One thing I love about this story is that, as Mary and the others wept and wished Jesus had come sooner, Jesus wept along with them. He wasn't crying from fear or because He thought that Lazarus would stay dead—He knew what was going to happen, after all. He wept out of love, sympathy, and compassion for his dear, grieving friends.

After He ordered the stone in front of the tomb to be moved out of the way—but just before it actually was moved—Jesus said something incredibly profound to Martha. "Did I not say to you that if you believe, you will see the glory of God?"

They removed the stone, and Jesus thanked God for hearing His prayer. Then He called Lazarus, who was still in his grave clothes, to come out of the tomb. And he did! He was alive again!

While his story was fairly unique in those days, throughout the Bible, God actually raised several people from the dead. The son of the Zarephath widow, the son of the Shunammite widow, the son of the Nain widow, a man who was buried in Elisha's grave, Jairus' daughter, Dorcas, Eutychus—all brought back to life after dying. And when Jesus rose from the dead Himself, countless saints rose from their graves as well!

Unbelievable? Perhaps. But I, for one, choose to believe it.

The Bolivian doctors said that Daniel was not out of the woods. He couldn't talk or walk. He had bounced along the gravel on his head, and the extent of his brain damage was unknown. Though they didn't say it, I was well aware we were not in a state-of-the-art hospital or a country known for unlimited resources and groundbreaking medical procedures. We were all just doing the best we could.

A few days later, Daniel was talking. We went to see him, and he could only say one word: *Sí*. Our conversations were somewhat limited, but he continued barking out that gravelly syllable in answer to questions. He was communicating—and his brain was keeping up with us.

About a week later, Daniel was home from the hospital and back in my Sunday school class, though still partially wrapped in bandages. That little boy, the one doctors said might never walk again, was running around so much that I had to tell him to sit down and behave. But my heart soared. He was alive, thinking, and running!

We were still a bit in shock when we talked to a group at the church who seemed grateful but not very surprised by this event. "God raised him from the dead!" my husband exclaimed. "Isn't that so incredible?"

"Yes," they told us, "but he is not the first. There was another. He was dead for a lot longer." We found out that the other man's dead body actually had been carried into the church building for a memorial service before his resurrection. Daniel, on the other hand, had been dead only for a little while.

After Jesus healed Lazarus, the Bible notes two reactions. People either believed in Jesus, or they tried to stop Him from continuing His ministry of healing and helping. It's no different today. Some see inexplicable wonders and believe. Some see, but push against Him. We all have a choice, and mine is to believe.

Another little boy, much younger than Daniel, lived perhaps two miles from him, through a maze of dusty roads, stray chickens, barbed wire, and concrete houses with outdoor sinks. Their families weren't friends, but they were all friends of mine. So, we all crossed paths from time to time.

When this second boy was born, there were some serious complications. I was in the United States at the time, but I heard from his aunt that he had seizures and eating issues, and he almost died more than once. He had surgery on his intestine, but his chances of survival seemed weak.

A few months later, his family was worried because he was alive, but not thriving. He was having fewer seizures and fevers, but they were still happening and seemed serious. And he often couldn't eat. A return trip to the children's hospital led to the scheduling of another surgery.

I was back in South America by this time, so I rushed to the hospital to see what I could do. Knowing how long the waits could be, I brought snacks and clean clothes for the baby's mother who would be there for hours.

When I arrived, I had no proof of any connection to the baby's family. I was not a relative, and even though the mother and aunt wanted me there, I had no evidence of that as I tried to enter the ward.

"What is the baby's name?" the hospital official quizzed me.

Name? I realized that I didn't know. The boy was about eight months old now, but very ill. As is common among Bolivian highlander families, they hadn't even named him yet. If he survived until his first birthday, then they would grant him a name. But how did they register him?

I bluffed, drawing myself up to look important and trying to speak without hesitation. "Josecito Paricahua," I said. "Son of José and Carmen." Basically, I had just called him by a youthful version of his father's name, hoping that his parents might have done the same.

They checked the chart. "We have a 'Baby Paricahua, mother Carmen,' " they said. "No first name. You may go in."

Josecito later became his name.

I visited with José and Carmen briefly and then went to speak privately with a doctor before the surgery began. Sometimes, medical personnel would speak to missionaries when they wouldn't speak to the patients or parents themselves. I wanted to know the baby's prognosis.

The surgeon's answer was not encouraging. "His chance is between very small and none," he told me.

My heart and hope felt deflated as the doctor rushed into surgery to try and save this tiny boy's life. During the course of all of this drama, the doctor confided in me something he perhaps should not have. He suspected an error in a previous operation—a nick in the intestines—had caused the child to become septic, leaking toxins into his body. That explained the fevers, the seizures, and the lack of appetite. After so many days, it was possible the damage was irreparable.

I stayed with the parents for four hours outside that surgical suite. We shared a concrete bench in a garden in front of those doors. Despite our vigilance there, no one came out to see us. We expected the surgery to last about two hours, but as time ticked on, I began to lose hope that he would beat the odds again.

Two-and-a-half hours passed, then three. Still we sat.

At one point, the doctor walked out of the suite—head down, mask still on. He took in our upturned, expectant faces, but simply shook his head and turned away, walking fast.

My heart broke.

I kept waiting for someone to come out and tell us what had happened, but the minutes kept ticking by with no word. Why didn't they come out? Why hadn't the doctor spoken to us? Where was Josecito? Was he dead or alive—or still struggling somehow in between? What could I say to these parents?

We had been praying off and on all day, together and silently. But now, I dropped my head into my clasped hands and prayed like my friend, Ana, had prayed. I felt God speaking to my soul. "Pray for life," the Holy Spirit prompted me. Was I brave enough to pray for life — to hear a doctor or nurse say Josecito was gone and still put my hand on a lifeless child and pray for his healing? In that moment, I knew I was. God would give me strength, because He was the one Who was asking me to do it. If He answered, we would praise Him. If He chose to not restore Josecito's life on this earth, He was God, and that was His right.

But I would obey.

I realized that, despite my faith — despite my ardent belief in His power to do miracles — I had God in a box. Maybe it wasn't as tight and constricting as the box the man searching for a million-dollar miracle used, but I had my limits, nonetheless. I believed that God raised people from the dead in the Bible and that people in foreign countries like India and Turkey sometimes saw it happen when they prayed in faith. Even so, I doubted that He would call me to witness it or pray for it.

Yet He did.

Finally, around the four-hour mark, a woman came out of those thick white hospital doors. When she pulled down her mask, there was a smile behind it. "Your baby is fine," she said.

Oh, may I never again try to cram the Almighty God of the universe into boundaries of my own making!

We celebrated Josecito's birthday that year under a cerulean sky, in a yard full of friends and balloons. There was a cake and a piñata and lots of toys. We celebrated his life differently than we celebrated most one-year-olds, because we knew how fragile our hold on it was.

I still don't know what happened in the surgical room that day. No one ever spoke to me about it. Perhaps it went smoothly and the doctor was shaking his head in amazement. Maybe he just had a stiff neck from the long, grueling operation. Perhaps it had been touch-and-go and things finally worked out well for us in the end. Possibly Josecito had died on that table and was resuscitated. I have no idea — in Bolivian hospitals, the full story often goes untold.

But I don't need to know because it wasn't just about Josecito. It was about all of us.

God could have stepped in to save the baby months before. But because He loved us, He had things to teach us through this experience. Josecito's parents grew in their faith and in their love for their son, while my view of God got a whole lot bigger.

And I would rather have that than a hundred million dollars.

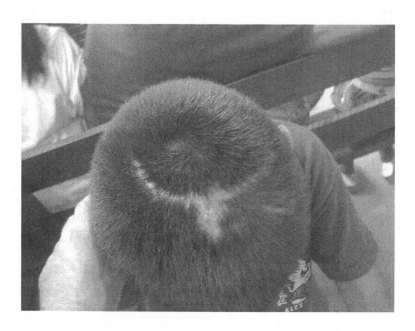

Daniel could see his scarred torso in the mirror, but not the wound on the top of his head. So after it had been mending for a while, he asked Tom to photograph it and show him. The scar always reminded Tom of the Texas Longhorns! God continues to do remarkable things in the life of Daniel, who became a church musician.

CANASTAS

By Janine

C HRISTMAS WAS DRAWING CLOSER AND *closer. Temperatures were rising on the southern half of the earth, and we once again traded pants and tennis shoes for shorts and sandals. City plazas and parks boasted stunning light displays, from giant angels to a house for Santa that was built from plastic, two-liter bottles. The markets swelled with crowds, searching and spending. Vendors sold plastic trees, with plastic ornaments to go on them and plastic toys to go beneath them.*

We had planned weeks ahead for our sons' Christmas presents, knowing that prices would rise in December and certain items could become hard to find. We had gifts for each one, but as Jesus's birthday approached, we decided we had a bit more shopping to do.

Fifteen girls we had met in an orphanage years before were now coming to my house once a week. These young ladies were no longer the little girls I first knew them as — almost all were in their late teens or early twenties, and the majority were now mothers themselves. We would chat and sip soft drinks as their children played at our feet or nursed and slept in their arms.

It was not an easy road for these women. Sadly, only a few had faithful, hardworking husbands. Most had boyfriends who came in and out of the picture. Money was very tight. Some of the women worked at respectable jobs when they could, serving as maids, store clerks, or office workers. But it was a constant struggle to pay their bills and keep themselves and their babies fed.

Where we lived, there is a tradition of Christmas canastas, or gift baskets that employers give to employees at the end of the year. They typically include snacks, household items, and a bottle of wine. I wanted to give the young women who came to our house each week something to help them through the holidays. I wanted to buy them each a kind of canasta.

We had never done that before. Why would we? These women didn't work for us; maybe they would even be offended. Nevertheless, the thought kept returning, and I had a feeling that they would be thrilled. So I began to dream. Tailor-made for their needs, our canastas would be a little different than the usual employer gifts. Instead of fruitcake and wine, I would include necessities such as laundry soap and cubes of dehydrated soup stock.

There was a problem, though. Monthly donations to our ministry had been falling for months, and our finances were tight. We sometimes struggled to pay our own bills. Fifteen girls meant fifteen baskets, fifteen rolls of toilet paper, fifteen bottles of cooking oil, fifteen sacks of sugar, fifteen bags of flour... Where would we come up with all that money?

Yet the idea nagged me day after day. Some of the girls were in serious straits that December, and their morale was low. Christmas for their children was looking bleak. We wanted to help.

Tom and I prayed for wisdom. How could we have such a strong desire to give these gifts to them and yet not have any means to carry it out?

Very shortly after our quiet, private prayer, a representative from our mission office in the States messaged us. A church in California had sent us a gift.

Almost to the penny, it was exactly what we needed to provide baskets for those fifteen young women and their children.

Joyfully, we shopped and packed the baskets. Joyfully, the women received them. One girl was especially moved — she said that getting a basket felt like someone had affirmed all the work she was doing as a mom to raise her child well. We celebrated together with hugs, photos, and even a few tears.

God knows what His children need before we even ask and He always has the means to provide it.

CHAPTER FOUR

PURPOSE: A MASTER MECHANIC

By Tom

W E LOVED OUR JOBS IN Latin America. When I was turning wrenches to make sure an airplane was safe to fly or when Janine was teaching a classroom full of children, we felt like we were right where we were supposed to be. We worked hard, but we were passionate about what we were doing.

I'll admit, though, that we really looked forward to those times when teams of people from the United States came to visit us. These groups helped with ministry projects that we didn't have money or manpower to do on our own. They carried mail for us. They helped drive away some of the homesickness we felt as a result of being separated from family and friends. Also, when we had guests around, we often got to schedule time off work and do things we usually didn't do, such as having dinner at a touristy restaurant or lounging around in a swimming pool.

After we'd been in Bolivia for about two years, we were visited by a family whose members were much more excited at the prospect of getting their feet wet in ministry projects than they were about getting them wet in a swimming pool.

I met Laura many years ago while I was in the US Coast Guard. She was a nursing student and became an encouraging friend. Through the years that followed, she married a pilot-mechanic named Renner and gave birth to two boys. One day, after a series of remarkable events in her life, she called to let me know that she and Renner wanted to bring their sons to Bolivia, visit my family, and see what our mission did firsthand.

Their visit was not intended to be a vacation. They wanted to see the area served by our aviation program and catch a vision for what God was doing there. They wanted to get dirty, to go places tourists don't usually go.

Janine and I decided to take them out to Roboré, a small, rural town in eastern Bolivia near the Brazilian border. A highway connecting Roboré to our city was finally under construction after years of unkept political promises. But it was still quite a drive, and most people chose to get there by train.

Our plan was to show our friends the town and highlight some of the needs of the people there. Then we would fly out in a mission plane to nearby San Fernando, a village with thatched-roof huts, no electricity, and piranhas in the river. We hoped to visit a group of children in a church there and spend time with a Bolivian friend who was their Sunday school teacher.

There were ten of us making the trip, including the visiting family, our family, our pilot (Alonso), and a Bolivian pastor named Timoteo. That was too many people for the long road trip in our truck and too many to fit in either of our mission's airplanes. So we chose to send two adults and four children in the plane with Alonso, and two other adults with me in our Land Cruiser.

Taking a ground vehicle was a good idea because it would give us a way to get around town and allow Alonso and Timoteo to stay and work for a few days longer after the rest of us left. They could fly back, and eight of us could return by land. So, off we went. The ground crew left hours earlier, and the flight crew soared over our heads about two-thirds of the way along, somewhere around the town of San Jose de Chiquitos.

The 400-kilometer (250-mile) trip toward Roboré was rather eventful for both groups. The journey by air only took about two hours. But those who flew had to avoid a storm, and the related turbulence brought about a lot of airsickness. When they arrived at the hotel, Janine took the boys—who were restless after being cooped up in the plane so long—into one room to play. Then the storm they had avoided arrived with fury, and she discovered that the roof of their lodging was full of holes. The tile floor, freshly-made bed, suitcases, four boys, and Janine all got an unwelcome shower.

I drove the ground team, and we traveled about eleven hours. The road we were on was laden with ridges like an old-fashioned washboard. It snaked back and forth over sections of highway construction the majority of the way. The bumps took their toll on all of us, including our beloved Land Cruiser. Both rear shocks were ripped from the chassis by the constant thrashing. After we arrived in the town, I took them off completely and found a local welder who could repair them.

We spent a few days in Roboré. Then, Alonso took Janine, Philip, and the visiting family out to the village, where they met with the church kids as planned. Janine and Laura also did a couple of unscheduled medical assessments, since Laura was a nurse. Alonso traveled to yet another small settlement further out, for a medical emergency. Meanwhile, I stayed with Peter and worked on getting the vehicle put back together for round two of the beating it would take to get us back to the city.

When the time came for the eight North Americans to make the return trip, we said goodbye to Alonso and Pastor Timoteo and piled into the truck—four adults and four little boys. We headed back the same way we had come, across the scrub brush of this piece of the South American Pantanal.

Just outside of town, there was a river. We had crossed it days before without much of a problem, except for a few moments in high water that obscured the headlights. The water in the center of the river had been just deep enough to cover them.

I didn't realize how much the river had swollen from the storm that had rolled through. When we crossed this time, the water came up over the hood and splashed the windshield. We prayed for protection as water seeped in from the cracks around the bottoms of the doors. We thanked God for four-wheel drive after we got to the other side.

Hours passed as we continued our journey without seeing many signs of civilization. We traveled mile after mile of slick, muddy road.

Various farmers had painted names on old tires and hung them from trees near the entrances to their farms. I joked with the boys that they were real rubber trees, growing tires in plain sight. We talked, sang, ate crackers, and played as many traveling games as we could think of that didn't require license plates or road signs.

With about two hours of traveling left until we got home, I gently pushed on the brakes to slow for a curve. Instead of the usual resistance, the pedal went to the floor! There was no traffic anywhere in sight, and the dirt highway was fairly level in that spot. So I coasted to a stop right in the middle of the road to assess the damage.

It was readily apparent that the front brake line had broken, and that with every push of its pedal, we were losing valuable fluid. Usually our truck was well-stocked with tools and emergency items. But this time, the toolkit had been left behind by mistake. We had no extra brake fluid with us to replace what was being lost.

Our only viable option was to pinch off the broken copper tube and hobble home with brakes on three of our four wheels. With the Leatherman Super Tool I always wore on my belt, Renner and I bent and pinched and flattened the end of that tube until we thought it would seal. With Renner underneath the Land Cruiser's carriage looking for leaks, I sat in the driver's seat again and pushed on the pedal.

It was still dripping. We tried again and again. With all our strength and that great tool, we could not seal off the tube.

During a quick look around, we found two round stones in the middle of the road, about the size of softballs. Smashing the tube between those two rocks finally sealed off the brake line and allowed us to get back on the road. We limped home a little slower and a little wiser.

After our trip was over and the truck was repaired the right way, I began to think about our adventure. What would I have done differently? What other tools or supplies should I have brought? What did God teach me?

The truth is that He taught me something that hit me hard and has stuck with me ever since.

Through the years, I have met and worked with some extraordinary people. At times, I found myself wondering why God would use me to work for Him. I didn't feel like anything special. Sometimes, I felt as if others had so much more talent and ability than I did—that they should have been the ones that He used in Bolivia, not me.

I came there as a mechanic. Not a pilot or pilot-mechanic, "just" a mechanic. People often reminded me of that when I told them what I did for a living. "Just a mechanic? You don't fly?"

Nope. I'm just a mechanic.

Many years before, God allowed me to meet a man named Marvin who was just a mechanic like I was. He was doing great things—being faithful to do his job, not anyone else's. Watching him helped me to see merit and purpose in my own calling as well.

God used our brake-line adventure to remind me, yet again, that He is in charge, and He had called me to serve Him in a particular way. He let me know that He is the Master Mechanic, not me. And He gets to choose what tools He wants to use.

Yes, there are super tools out there that may be able to get the job done faster or better, in theory. But He needs tools that are yielded and willing to do what He wants them to do. At times, I may feel like one of those rocks that we used to smash the brake line together on the dusty road from Roboré. I look around and see others who are better equipped, stronger, and more impressive—like my Leatherman. I can feel dull and ordinary sometimes, as if I were nothing special.

Yet the Master Mechanic chose to use me, and He still does. In His hands, timing, and way, I become just the right man for the job.

When we crossed the river on our trip, there was definitely no getting out to take a picture! But there were plenty of other times we encountered flooded roadways in Bolivia, including the day we saw this very large mudpuddle on a soggy street. Trucks driving across it caused significant waves as they passed by.

LOST

By Janine

O UR TRIP TO ROBORÉ HAD *been challenging but also very good. We were leaving with hearts and minds full of happy memories and hope.*

We had a problem, however. We couldn't exactly find the way home.

After leaving the pilot and plane with Alonso and Timoteo, we got back into the Land Cruiser and pointed it in the direction of the highway. But as we rode out of the small town, we got a bit lost. Every time we made a turn, we were met with a dead end or a wandering dirt trail. Signs just seemed to lead us further astray from our goal.

There were eight of us in the truck, plus luggage. We felt hot, crowded, and a little frustrated. Then we saw a man on the side of the road who looked like he wanted to talk to us.

He was a funny sort of man, from the unusual way he conversed with us to the way he was dressed — in natty, but outdated, plaid pants. I'll admit that I wasn't sure about letting him too close. But he definitely seemed to be at home in the town and assured me that he could pull us out of the circles in which we had been traveling.

He told us he knew exactly where we needed to go. He said he was sure of it. Then he gestured toward the way from which we had just come.

"That's it!" he told us. "That's the way you want to go to get out of town."

Tom had his doubts. "Are you sure?" he asked the man. "I thought it was the other way."

The man in the plaid pants nodded emphatically. "Definitely," he said. "The highway is just across that water."

There was a little creek of sorts, running full after a hard rain. It wasn't the mighty river we would have to cross on our trip home, but it was substantial.

"Across that? Are you sure?"

Tom hesitated.

"Positive!" the man told him. "I will go with you."

We had little room left inside the vehicle, and something still seemed wrong to me. So Tom told the man to hop on the running board outside of my passenger door instead of squeeze in with us. He happily obliged, firmly planting his feet.

With my window open, we chatted a bit as Tom drove down the dirt road, then we held on tight as we bumped and sloshed through the running water of the creek. The man descended on the other bank, looking quite happy.

We looked around, eager to head home.

"Sir," we asked him, "where is the highway? We don't see any signs."

He pointed back the way we had just come, in the direction we had been going before meeting him.

"That way?" we asked, incredulous. "But why did you tell us it was this way?"

He shrugged before turning to walk off, carrying his fancy-pants self away from us and our truck.

"I wanted a ride across the water."

CHAPTER FIVE

PEACE: WRESTLING WITH FEAR

By Janine

"**A**REN'T YOU SCARED?"
It was a question we heard over and over as we prepared to move overseas. So many people expected us to fear life in Bolivia. They wondered aloud about our choice to live among giant insects, reckless drivers, required immunizations, and government instability.

Believe it or not, I didn't spend all my time being afraid.

Don't get me wrong. I certainly wasted too much time fretting and worrying. As someone who typically wears my heart on my sleeve, I expressed that worry and fretfulness far too often. But in my heart, I wasn't terrified the way some people seemed to expect.

Then our second term came, and I got a lot more acquainted with fear.

First, I had a problem with blood vessels in both of my legs. I spent part of one Christmas week on my back, barely able to walk. That was followed by salmonella and a bout of appendicitis for Peter; a seriously damaged ankle for Tom; and two concussions, a broken thumb, and a hospital stay for Philip.

In the midst of these health concerns, the country of Bolivia also was in turmoil. A new president had come into power and was drawing emotional lines in the sand. The country was polarized between support for him in his highland capital city of La Paz and the lowland government in our own city, which was fighting for autonomy. People spoke of civil war and violence. There were intense demonstrations and people disappearing in the dark of night.

I also was dealing with some challenges at work. Ministering to children in need in Bolivia had become quite difficult, as I saw some of the most vile child abuse cases of all my time as a teacher and child advocate.

As potentially frightening as these situations were, however, I think my deep fear didn't start until after my first case of dengue fever, a debilitating, mosquito-borne illness that is common in tropical areas like ours was.

Tom and I contracted our first case of dengue fever on the very same day. Less than a year later, I was hit with a second strain of that same virus. Months after that, when I felt the symptoms for a third time, I skipped the blood test and just stayed in bed. I knew the treatment options, and there weren't many—acetaminophen, fluids, food, and rest. In my mind, I heard other people's words echo back to me that most people don't live long enough to get dengue fever three times. Apparently, I am an exception.

Shortly after the first bout, we helped host a work team from the East Coast. They were mostly dedicated, big-hearted college and high-school students, hardworking and generous. The mission guest house was already full when they arrived, so this team stayed at a nearby hotel. We stopped by there each day to provide transportation. Sometimes, that meant hired buses or taxis. Other times, it meant friends' vehicles and our Land Cruiser.

In those days, we were in the habit of doing what we called the "Bolivian Squeeze," which allowed as many people into our vehicle as wanted to ride with us. Most Bolivians don't own their own cars, nor do they want to pay bus and taxi fares. So our friends often would ask to pile into our vehicle if we were traveling their way. Our back seatbelts were broken, but laws in that region didn't require backseat seatbelts at all. We packed in as many as twenty-two people at a time in that truck. It was crazy.

I usually rode in the front next to Tom. But on one particular day with the East Coast work team, I decided to sit somewhere else. It was only a five-minute drive from the hotel to the mission base. Our guests were mostly tall, broad-shouldered North American guys who were unaccustomed to the Bolivian Squeeze. There were about ten of us, and I wanted to be hospitable and generous. So I volunteered to ride with my children in the seat farthest back, a tight, confined space that we entered and exited either by waiting for the truck to empty or by using the cargo door.

I don't like small spaces like that and often get car sick. But it was a short ride, so I thought I'd be okay. With our legs tucked in tight, I put my arms around my sons' shoulders and sang and chatted with them, enjoying the trip.

No problem, no complications.

About two months after that, I was with a different work team. We were in a squatters' camp on the outskirts of town and had just finished a class with a lovely group of lively children. While Tom began to load up people and supplies, I continued chatting with some of the adults from the village, helping them sell their handicrafts to our North American friends.

It wasn't a big surprise that I was the last to arrive back at the truck. What *was* a surprise was that our truck was the only vehicle still there. The others had left with minimal passengers in them, and all the remaining team members were squeezing into our Toyota.

They had left me a spot in the back seat, and I climbed through the cargo door and over the seatback to get in position. But a few things were different this time. Instead of my two sons, I was sitting with one of my best friends and her daughter. Instead of seven young men in front of us, there were men, women, and children with bags and boxes of supplies. Our trip would be twenty or thirty minutes, not five.

All this seemed relatively reasonable. I had been in similar situations before. So why was such a frenzy rising in me?

I glanced behind me and saw empty space between me and the cargo door. It was an easy way out, just in case. I took a deep breath and began to relax into the cushions. Then the door opened and someone put one last stack of boxes inside, blocking that exit.

I was trapped. Panic set in.

To this day, I don't know what had changed. Perhaps God was doing a spiritual work in me, dealing with issues of trust and worry. Maybe something physiological had happened.

During my first round of dengue fever, I lost a considerable amount of weight—about twelve pounds. My skin had gone through the infamous rash stage that often accompanies the end of the illness. I had experienced delusions. By the time this second work team arrived, I also had lost a considerable amount of my thick, long hair. I hadn't told many people, as it wasn't very noticeable yet. My hair had been shocked and deadened by the fever, though, and it was falling out in handfuls.

Was it possible that dengue had scarred my psyche as well? That, while the outward effects had nearly disappeared, some of the irrational apprehension remained? Maybe I was feeling residual effects even weeks later. I don't know. What I do know is that day began about a year-and-a-half of panic attacks, mostly in claustrophobic situations.

I found myself unable to sit in the back seat of the truck even when it was empty. I took a ride in one of our six-seat mission planes and found myself crying quietly as we flew, wondering how I would survive if we crashed.

What was wrong with me?

I didn't know the answer to that, but on some level, I knew this: God was going to have to take me deeper in my faith, because things were not well with my soul.

I told only three people about what was happening in my heart—Tom, and my friends Dan and Jenny. Jenny had been sitting with me in the back seat of the truck the day my panic attacks began—the one who quietly helped me get reseated in the front.

She also was the friend who traveled with me to Chicago a few months later. During this season of my life, I was directing our Children's Ministry Team in Bolivia, which was reaching out to hundreds of children and scores of teachers. Jenny was a vital part of that program. She and I heard about a conference for children's ministry workers at Willow Creek Community Church in Illinois. We got permission from our bosses to travel north and attend this useful event, with its powerfully relevant classes and seminars. I was excited to go, but on the long jet ride there — as I flew farther and farther from my husband and children — fear often welled up inside me.

Little did I know that God's agenda for me that week included more than learning better ways to teach children and teachers. He had more in mind than giving my friend and me tools for our job and time with each other. He had a direct message for me about my struggle with fear.

At the conference, I attended a session by author and editor Christine Yount Jones titled, "Erase Your Fears," in which she talked about "worst-case scenarios."[5] In context, she was referring to the way many people believe they should embark on a great outreach to benefit others — such as building a children's program — and may even have the tools to do so, but are scared to begin. However, the intensely personal experience that she shared as an example was not about starting a new outreach or ministry. It was about the death of her husband.

Christine's worst-case scenario was that her husband might die and leave her. This nightmare came true in an instant, while they were on a romantic snowmobiling trip together.

Her story — the circumstances that laid the groundwork for her advice to us — gave her the right to be heard. And her message changed my life.

She taught me to lean into my fears and say, "If so, so what?" If I don't get what I want, if things don't go as I planned, if I have to face my own worst-case scenarios — then what? Am I still going to believe God is capable and knows what He is doing? Am I still going to face that hard thing and survive it? Is it going to be okay for me?

Those questions are hard, but they're also game changers.

I can't tell you I wasn't terrified to get back on that plane,

---

5 Yount-Jones, Christine. "Erase Your Fears." Speech, Conspire 2008, Willow Creek Community Church, South Barrington, Illinois, April 23, 2008.

because I was. But in Christine's session, I began to realize something that shaped me and allowed me to heal. My heavenly Father is all-powerful, and He loves me. He knows my innermost thoughts (including how much I fought fear during that time). He cares for me even more than I love my own children. So there was no way He would allow me to die the way I feared most, unless it somehow fit into His sovereign plan.

Unless that kind of hardship was for my good and revealed some of His perfect glory, He would never permit it. Because of those truths, I could lean into it. It either wouldn't happen, or it would happen for a powerfully good reason. Therefore, the most appropriate thing to do was trust Him with a grateful heart.

I began to say to myself, ¿Y que? — the Spanish version of, "And if so, so what?"

I experienced great healing over the next few months as I rested on this newfound knowledge of God's character and sovereignty. He had been faithful to care for me for more than 13,500 days so far. Could I not trust Him with the next day... and the one after that?

Another profound step in my healing process was sandwiched between many prayers for a lasting peace from this emotional struggle. One day, about a year after the first attack, I again found myself crammed into the back of a vehicle — actually in the hatchback space — among children and supplies. Jenny's husband, Dan, was driving that day and knew that I was nervous. But options were limited and the front seat wasn't one of them this time.

Dan came to the back of the car and quietly shared a prayer from the Bible that he taught his three daughters to keep them from fear: "Whenever I am afraid, I will trust in You (God)" (Ps. 56:3, New King James Version). I recited those words in my mind over and again on that ride and during the next few days. Almost before I knew it, the panic attacks were gone.

Despite my best efforts, I didn't have words of my own that could defeat the fear. Yet in those moments, as I leaned on God's words, I realized they were strong enough to hold me.

One of the final events that helped me to rest again and let go of my worry involved the growing unrest in Bolivia.

Late in 2008, the situation looked particularly bleak. There had been rioting, arson, looting, and lies. There had been threats against our children's school and hundreds of local evacuations. Americans were leaving in droves. The American embassy told us that Marines were standing by if we needed transportation out of the country. In the weeks ahead, a pastor would be murdered by police. I occasionally heard and saw a military-style helicopter flying over our neighborhood. Rumors were abundant and wild.

Our mission's leaders offered everyone on our crew airplane tickets to fly back to their base in Florida. Eventually, all our single women were required to leave. Our family was given the opportunity to stay if we wanted to, though, and we did.

Tom and I weren't afraid, nor were our kids. They wanted to stay.

Demonstrations and threats cancelled school and work some days. We were concerned, frustrated, worried, tired, interrupted, and bewildered about what to do in the day-to-day pressure cooker in which we were living. But our family still wasn't very scared that we would be injured by the fighting around us.

One night, I had been asked to summarize the rapidly changing situation for some of our leadership team in the States. That meant listening to various broadcasts — which expressed propaganda from both sides — to try and discover the truth that was consistent across the various stations. I listened for about three hours, taking notes in a combination of Spanish and English. Just before I went to bed, something on one of the newscasts grabbed my attention.

Hugo Chavez, the Venezuelan president at the time, was showing off two Russian warplanes that were temporarily parked in his country. He emphatically stated his personal offense at the way Bolivian lowlanders (among whom we lived) were speaking against his friend and their president, Evo Morales. He threatened to use the Tu-160 bombers against our city if he felt it was necessary.

Tom and I didn't take that too seriously. In fact, I'll admit that we smirked a little that evening. Chavez often made dramatic and derogatory remarks. He was the one who called a high-ranking Catholic official a clown and implied our US president at the time was the devil. Chavez was a big talker. We went to sleep that night concerned for our guest country and unsure what the next day would bring. But we were fairly sure we were in for a good night's rest and had little to fear from *Presidente* Hugo Chavez.

We awoke to an explosion of light and sound.

I instantly thought of the curious helicopter that had been circling our backyard and of Chavez' menacing words about attacking our city from the air. Tom bolted to the window for a better idea of what was going on and I ran—fearful—down the hall to my sons' bedroom.

In those moments, as I ran, the realization hit me: I couldn't save them from a bomb. It was entirely out of my hands.

The Bible says that a man makes his plans, but God orders that man's steps. How true that was on that night. We could have had our suitcases packed, emergency documents ready, and three escape routes and contingency plans in place. All the necessary and wise decisions could have been made. At the end of the day, though, we were completely reliant on God's mercy and grace.

I couldn't protect my kids from everything. Could I truly protect them from anything?

When I reached them, I found them sleeping soundly in their beds, undisturbed. I prayed over them, smiled over them, and then heard Tom call to me from our room.

Lightning, not bombs, had struck our city. In fact, such intense lightning and thunder burst around us that some nationals later told me they believed God was sending a message.

I went back to bed, shaken. I fell back to sleep the only way I knew how. It was the way my mother had taught me when I was a child—the way God had been reteaching me as I wrestled with fear.

I poured out my heart to my heavenly Father. I thanked Him for our safety and prayed for others I had heard of on the news—mothers in Afghanistan who couldn't reassure themselves that the flashes were just lightning, parents who couldn't hold their children and protect them from falling bombs. I finally understood a tiny piece of their pain—and it was terrifying. So I prayed God would shield and comfort them like He continued to shield and comfort us.

I fell asleep quickly and slept well that night.

I still fall asleep easily most nights—peacefully, and without fear. The panic attacks are all gone.

Beating fear has nothing to do with changing our circumstances. It's about keeping our eyes focused on Jesus.

In this sometimes-scary and crazy world, we want a strategy for overcoming fear. Positive thinking, health and exercise, uplifting friends, and chamomile tea all have their place, but they will only take us so far and only help us so much.

In the end, when there is no way we can handle things on our own, we come to realize that only God can bring true peace. Only He can calm our hearts completely. As I trust and lean on Him, listen to what He says, and pray my concerns back to Him, fear disappears.

Our family Christmas photo in 2007 included
our German shepherd, Turbo.

INSTINCT

By Janine

W HILE IN LANGUAGE SCHOOL IN Costa Rica, we didn't have a car. So, Tom and I walked to our morning classes – a mile one way, Our boys would take turns walking alongside of us, being carried, or being pulled in our red Radio Flyer wagon. Around noon, Tom accompanied Philip and me home and then went back to get our son Peter, whose classes lasted until 3 p.m.

It was a long walk for a two-year-old and a five-year-old, but we enjoyed the journey, often stopping to peruse the florist shop or buy a loaf of hot, braided, cinnamon-raisin bread from the bakery. We would talk about patterns in the sidewalk tiles, smile at puppies through the fences, or stop to touch the mimosa pudica plants at the park, watching their sensitive leaves curl up and shrink away from us.

One particular day, we were finally within sight of our house when we saw something new, right in plain view. It was a spectacular green caterpillar – not a deep, forest green, but brighter than a green apple. Its back was covered with magnificent projections that looked like the tips of redwood leaves, and there was a bright stripe extending from head to tail.

Naturally, my children wanted to play with it.

As they begged me to let them hold the fearsome-looking creature, my gut said an emphatic, "No!" But I had been spoken to that very day by a teacher who thought I was acting overprotective of my children in this new place. The tap water was contaminated, so I gave the boys bottled water. I cleaned their little hands frequently. I often reminded them not to touch the "pokies," which were everything from nails and barbed wire to crown of thorns plants and cacti. Broken concrete and rebar jutted up from the ground, and peeling sheets of rusted metal stuck out of slides and swings. It seemed like danger was everywhere we walked.

My language professor told me that I needed to loosen up — to let the children get dirty, drink the water, adapt.

"Let them be like the Costa Rican children," she told me.

I looked down at the little caterpillar, soft and squishy and gorgeously dressed. How could that small thing possibly hurt my kids?

I thought of visiting my grandfather's property in the country when I was a young girl. I remembered playing with siblings and cousins there, catching wooly bear caterpillars. We would gather them up, and they would curl into little doughnut shapes, their orange and black fur bristling along their backs. We would pet them gently, and the worst thing they ever did was mistake our hands for their restroom. What harm could a caterpillar bring? What would it do — bite them? Was that even possible? Did they have teeth?

My sense of logic won out, so I let my children pick up this marvelous creation. They petted it, and we took pictures with the camera we retrieved from the house. They oohed and aahed and grinned until we decided it was time to go.

"Can we keep it? Please?" the boys begged.

I wasn't sure how to answer. On one hand, it could be a great science and nature activity. It could be like a pet that we fed, watered, watched, and then released when it became a — a what, exactly? Would this thing become a butterfly? Was it actually a caterpillar, or just some kind of worm? I shuddered at the thought.

We were only about a block from our house, so I decided we would go home and do some Internet research before bringing the animal inside.

We walked in the door, and I immediately sent the boys to wash their hands well with soap and water. Like I said, I'd held enough caterpillars to know they could be, um, messy. And what if it secreted something toxic? Then I went to look for a name for the creature we had found.

The Internet service at our house was slow, and searching without the caterpillar in front of me was pretty difficult. "Green redwood leaf caterpillar" wasn't bringing up a lot of matches. But finally, I found it — an Io moth. I was letting my children play with the larvae of an Io moth. The description used terms like, "stinging spines," "venomous," "painful," and "can be fatal to persons who are allergic."

My next call was to our doctor.

Before our move, I had never heard of erucism, the word for injuries that can be caused by a caterpillar. (After leaving Costa Rica, we would see it firsthand. Tom received painful burns from the brush of a fuzzy gray Bolivian "burro" caterpillar.[6] His skin was marked for weeks.)

But my kids were absolutely fine. They had been cuddling up to an animal that has a reputation for striking at the faintest touch. God graciously spared them from that.

It's a balance, isn't it, listening to the wisdom and knowledge of others and also listening to that nudging voice inside?

Later, the instructor who had advised me to loosen up saw the pictures we had taken of that bright-green insect. Her eyes grew wide with surprise.

"Not that!" she said. "We would never let our children play with that!"

Good to know.

---

6 Megalopyge opercularis, or puss caterpillar.

Peter and Philip were overjoyed to discover the beauty
(and thankfully, not the danger) of an Io moth larva.

CHAPTER SIX

COMFORT: EXPERIENCING MEANING IN SUFFERING

By Janine

"In this world, you will have trouble. But take
heart! I have overcome the world."

— Jesus (John 16:33b NIV)

CALLS FROM GLADYS WERE FAIRLY common at my house
since her sister Rosa worked for me. Those calls had
become more serious, however, as Gladys underwent
tests and treatments for irritation and loss of vision in one eye. By
Christmas, she wore a patch. The problem seemed to be coming
from somewhere deep beyond the reach of an ophthalmologist.

When she telephoned a few days after the holiday to ask Rosa
to leave work and meet her at a neurologist's office, I had no idea
it would be the last time I heard her voice.

Rosa called a few hours later and explained that Gladys had
collapsed in the clinic while she was showing the specialist the
site of her pain. Unable to afford the luxury of an ambulance, Rosa
had hired a man with a truck to drive them to the hospital while
she performed CPR on her unconscious sister.

When I, along with other missionaries, caught up with her,
Gladys was lying on a bed in an otherwise-empty emergency

room. I watched as a janitor splashed pink antiseptic on the floor beneath her, then left without mopping it up. The strong, germicidal scent spread through the room as I helplessly waited for Gladys to respond or improve.

Despite closed eyes and stilled lips, she moved in obvious agitation. Her arm twitched so violently, in fact, that the pulse oximeter fell from her finger, and a creepy, flatline noise leaked through the room. Nurses watching an evening television show in their station bristled when I asked for help. If I wanted the sensor reattached, one groused, I should do it myself.

So we did it ourselves.

We stood in a group around Gladys, conversing quietly. I felt restless, as if I should be doing something to help, but I couldn't think of what that something might be. She had an aneurism, someone said. One of our missionary doctors explained that treatment for this would likely be risky even in the States. Surgery probably wouldn't be an option in her particular case. We had to just wait and see—and pray.

I stared out of the room toward the lobby. Near the front door, an artificial Christmas tree, for some unknown reason, had been assembled upside down. Its strange V shape, wide at the top and narrowing to a little point in its stand, made the whole event feel like something out of *The Twilight Zone*.

During the night, Gladys was moved to a different hospital with more attentive care. Nurses watched her diligently, and she was surrounded by monitors and equipment. While her room at the first hospital was just footsteps from the street, the intensive-care unit at this hospital was deep within a labyrinth of hallways, toward the back of a building. She was no longer the sole patient either—plenty of other beds were occupied.

Families ate, talked, or sat quietly in old plastic chairs in the enormous waiting room. A few people had come with bed linens or mats, ready to sleep on the concrete floor.

We still waited, prayed, and hoped for a sign of improvement in Gladys. Maybe she would tell us what she felt, or her eyelids would open and she would look up at us. Maybe her feet would walk out of that hospital.

But those things didn't happen.

On my birthday, about two days after Gladys's collapse in the neurologist's office, I was invited to a children's home where we occasionally volunteered. The giggly girls wouldn't tell me why I was being detained there, but it was no secret — they were throwing a surprise party for me. My heart was happy to see them, but I was desperate to be back with Gladys. During the lengthy celebration, while waiting for the cake to be frosted, I slipped out of the crowd for a few minutes and went back to the hospital.

Rosa grabbed my arm and told me that her sister, who remained on life support, was growing cold. She sensed a change. I visited Gladys and found her agitated like before, but much less so than on that first night. She still was unable to take a breath on her own. I talked to her, tried to touch her hand and the top of her head around the tubes, and prayed with her. Then I returned to the orphanage and attempted to put on a cheerful expression to match those of the girls.

They made me a late-night dinner and sang songs in my honor. They brought the cake they had made from scratch and pushed my face into it, as is the custom. I laughed with them, despite my divided feelings.

After another hour or so, my family and I were walking to the front gate, saying goodbye with the moon and stars overhead. Our cell phone rang. Gladys was gone. My husband and I smiled sadly at each other, thanked the crowd of girls who had worked so hard and given me so much attention for my birthday, and then raced home.

Tom took our sons inside, but I didn't even make it across the threshold. Two missionary women were outside the house, waiting to give me a ride back to the hospital. Upon arrival, we rushed through the glass doors and headed toward the maze of hallways leading to the ICU. In the entry hall, we passed a woman who was seated in a hard chair with her head bowed low. Her long, dark curls hung loose, covering her face like a curtain.

Something struck at my heart, and I dropped to my knees softly in front of her.

"Rosa?" She was nearly unrecognizable in her grief. I saw in her hand the green hair band she often wore to my house, the one that pinned her tresses up neat against her head. She raised her brown eyes to meet my blue ones, and I saw deep valleys of anguish.

In Bolivia, it is not a tidy matter to bury a loved one. The family and friends do much of the work themselves. I was grateful that the two other women who were there with me knew how to manage those details. They began making arrangements for embalmment, the purchase of a coffin, and the rental of a hearse. Rosa and I were left the job of claiming the body.

We waited in a darkened parking lot until two orderlies arrived, carrying the weight of something between them in a sheet. Respectfully but unceremoniously, they parted the material so we could see the face that had been so dear to us. I pulled my friend into my shoulder as we wept together over her sister's corpse.

"Yes, yes — that is her."

Highland funerals last three days, not three hours. I remember moments during those days like a series of snapshots. There was the strange shop of the embalmer. The sparkling green dress Gladys was buried in. The car ride behind the hearse that night. The stalk of wheat a friend added to the first funeral bouquet to signify the words written in John 12:24: "Truly, truly, I say to you, unless a grain of wheat falls into the earth and dies, it remains alone; but if it dies, it bears much fruit" (ESV).

Early in the morning, a crowd at the church shared a meal of *guiso* — a type of stew which was Gladys's favorite. Then we sang, sorrowfully but with hope, at the funeral service: "I have a home, home, beautiful home — beyond the sun."

I remember the walk with Rosa and Tom through a flooded cemetery to select an above-ground crypt. Deep, dirty water pulled so hard at my feet that it broke the leather strap of my sandal. Uncomfortable at the thought of what I was walking in, Tom lifted me up onto his back and carried me alongside rows of tall, thick walls holding sealed-over remains.

Then there was another walk — the long, hot one behind the

hearse on burial day—with me wearing black and solemnly holding the hand of Rosa's youngest daughter. There were the enormous sprays of flowers, heavy in the arms of the uncles. White disposable cups filled with soda, served graveside. The face of Gladys's son as he put roses on his mother's coffin.

The ancient Greek playwright Euripides wrote, "No mortal man comes through life unscathed." We surely didn't come through that week unscathed. By the time the formalities were finished, my heart felt as wrung out as a damp rag. I was just a friend, barely more than an acquaintance of Gladys's. How much deeper the bruising was for her sister, brother, nephew, nieces, and son.

Geography doesn't keep us from sorrow. There is plenty to go around, whatever continent we call home. My suffering did not begin or end inside Bolivian borders. But that was the place where I grappled with it most—the place where, amidst ugly circumstances, I wrestled with big "whys" and "what nows."

It was there that I searched for words of comfort after the drunken murder of a friend's husband and sons. It was there that I tried to keep breathing as I met with a child beaten so badly she lost not just her vision, but her whole eye.

I've sat at the bedside of a twelve-year-old who lost her father in a car wreck, and I've stood graveside while three babies wept for their mother. I have listened to the wails of a woman after the sudden death of her infant. I have held another woman in my arms after an abortion clinic took not only her child's life, but nearly her own.

I've listened to my son Peter ask if he would die, as we fought to stop the virus that ravaged his body. I've run down a foreign street in a strange city, clutching my children as we sought to escape an angry mob. I've pushed Philip toward the floorboards of a taxi as explosions sounded around us. I have grieved the loss of my tiny niece, Elizabeth, who lived and died in a California hospital while we were more than 5,000 miles away from her. I have faced so many illnesses and injuries in our family that I can't remember them all. I have said goodbye to pets, people, friendships, and three nations that I have called home.

I know there is suffering... and there is *suffering*. There are moments we can see a divine plan in our heartaches, and other moments when it seems no one has ever hurt as badly as we are hurting.

I get that.

And yet, I've found hope. Not trite, light, shifting hope. Solid, real hope that sustained me as I was walking through fire. In my darkest days, I learned some things that lifted the veil of grief and gave me a glimpse into the mystery of those haunting questions of why and what now?

During those most difficult times, I discovered a deep truth about our heartaches and sorrows — the ones that "just happen," the ones that we don't see coming, the ones that don't seem right or fair.

The truth is that God has a plan, and it is good. Because of this, we can trust Him.

It doesn't seem to make sense, does it? Life can be so hard, yet God is good? How can that be?

I love the moments when I get to see the plan and purpose unfold right away. At the end of a hard workweek, there is a welcomed paycheck. After nine months of pregnancy and hours of labor, there usually is a baby. At the end of long rehearsals, there are often ovations. At the end of tiring sports practices, there often are games won and even trophies and championships awarded. I love that.

In the same way, God sometimes brings quick, happy endings after suffering.

Sometimes.

I remember a story like that from my life. In my service as Children's Ministry Director in Bolivia, I usually worked within the city limits of Santa Cruz de la Sierra. On occasion, however, I would travel bumpy hours to villages, tiny towns, and rustic settlements to meet with teachers or children. Once I was invited to such a place, and I gathered a team of nationals from the city to help. I began preparing them for our adventure, during which they would instruct, feed, and entertain children while I trained rural teachers and parents.

Except for me, and a doctor who was graciously accompanying us to do free medical clinics, most of the team members were not used to traveling. But we definitely had enthusiasm on our side. We were working hard and eagerly looking forward to departure day. Tom and Philip were not able to make the journey with us, but Peter—who was about eleven at the time—was planning to come and help.

The day before our trip, I decided that Peter and I should go for medical checkups. He had been feeling ill, and there was a strange sensation and swelling in my legs. We would be on a train for about twenty-four hours, round trip, and working several days in a remote area. I thought that we should be cleared medically before leaving, just in case. So we went to see the doctor who was planning to accompany us on the trip.

It didn't take long to declare us grounded. Peter had a virus and needed care and rest at home. My circulatory system wasn't functioning properly, and the train ride could have led to blood clots and serious danger. Neither of us was fit to travel.

To say I was disappointed would be an understatement. I was deflated. The doctor's wife—who also was a doctor—assured me that God had a plan, and I needed to rest in it. In fact, her husband was in the middle of a very busy week and was struggling to get away for the trip as promised. God had a reason for this change in plans, she said.

I tried to get the rest of the team to carry on without me, but they were not yet ready to be at the helm. They protested and refused. So with extreme reluctance, I cancelled the plans.

How was this part of God's will? I fumed to myself. *People needed us. They had begged us to come. Arrangements were already made. And now my son was sick? I was injured? God could have prevented that, so why didn't He?*

The next day, with my legs worsening, I was home watching the news. To my great surprise, I saw that there had been a protest that morning. The very day we were to leave for our trip, a train trestle we would have crossed was pulled apart by an angry throng of demonstrators. Travel was halted. We could have been on those tracks, but God had put up roadblocks — as difficult and unfair as they seemed at the time — to stop us.

My son and my circulatory system both healed eventually. They were just "light and momentary troubles," as 2 Corinthians 4:17 calls them (NIV). And I was able to see, almost immediately, that God had been at work in our pain.

I know it's not always possible to see God's hand so quickly, but isn't it wonderful when it does happen? I remember being sick with my second or third strain of dengue fever. Instead of being in a room at the mission base with around-the-clock care like I had been the first time, I was home in my own bed. But in the moments before dawn, I was too uncomfortable to sleep. The sickness made me clumsy and awkward, and I didn't want to stumble and wake my family members who had been working hard during the day to care for me. So I lay very still, waiting for them to rise on their own or for sleep to return to me. In the quiet of those early morning hours, God revealed something very precious.

I am not a morning person. With the exception of sick children, fishing trips, and airplane departures, almost nothing gets me out of bed before 6 a.m. — definitely not sunrises. I have seen too many sunsets to count. I've also seen late-morning winter sunrises in the United States. But intentionally waking up early to watch a sunrise? That's really not normal behavior for me.

As I lay there that day, desperately longing for sleep, I saw signs of morning fill my picture window. Dawn did not come with the dusky gray and warm pink light I expected, however. The palm trees and other plants in our backyard weren't blurred, dim versions of themselves. They were crisp, black silhouettes, as sharp in their edges as cardboard cutouts. Behind them, growing increasingly more brilliant, was a sky aflame. Not just orange and yellow, but tangerine, apricot, gold, and rose. Its vibrancy, fronted by the blackness of the vegetation, made the landscape as surreal as a movie set.

I had been so frustrated and whiny in my illness. Yet now,

with my gaze frozen to the window in front of me, I was simply awestruck. I thought about waking my tired husband and sons so they could see this dazzling display. But I barely dared to move. It was as if the scene would dissipate with the slightest motion, like a beautiful dream fading away.

In those breathtaking moments, I realized that I would have missed this spectacular beauty if I had not been exactly where I was: aching so much on my sickbed that I could not sleep. My husband, children, and friends could not see it. I would have slept right through it if given the chance. But my pain brought me right to the place of glory.

Later, as I realized that my illness had brought me more than a nice sunrise, I wrote about it on my blog:

> This week, I have had dengue fever... But you know what? Without the suffering of this week, there are multiple blessings I would have missed. For instance, Philip sitting next to my bed, his legs still not long enough to reach the floor, reading me chapters out of the Bible because he thought I might want to hear that. The cards he made for me. The sweet little kisses snuck in when I told him to not get too close in case I had a different, contagious virus. Peter, sitting beside me, calling the doctor, holding my hand, and telling me "I love you." I love yous don't come often from my nearly teenage son, and I cherish each one. My husband took time off work to sit with me, even though there was nothing he could "do" to make me feel better. He hates to miss work and sit still, and I know that. But he sat hours with me, reading to me, brushing the knots out of my hair, making sure I kept drinking sips of Gatorade... He is something amazing...
>
> ...If I hadn't have been sick... I might not have been lying still and quiet when the wind rolled—I

don't know how else to explain it—through those trees one night, sounding so much like waves on an ocean. I might not have been reminded of a song my mom wrote many years ago based on Isaiah 26:3, "Thou wilt keep him in perfect peace, whose mind is stayed on Thee: because he trusteth in Thee" (King James Version). "I might not have called her—and I so needed to hear her voice.

Beautiful moments this week—and they came about because of suffering... I wouldn't have chosen the painful things if God had not set them out before me... But I have learned not to run from suffering either. Because He works *all* things—even painful things—for our good."[7]

Author Luci Swindoll once said, "You can't know health unless you have been sick. You can't know victory unless you've known loss. You have no basis of comparison unless you've experienced opposites."[8]

I may not want it to be true, but our world needs suffering. I (gulp) need suffering.

In it, we see the protection, purpose, and pull of Providence, leading us. It is the foil by which we see compassion, comfort, healing, and selflessness. As I dealt with twelve deaths in my first two years on the mission field, I learned more deeply to live for what mattered. After being betrayed by others, I learned how God's faithfulness really is enough. In the imposed slowing down due to illnesses, injury, and loss, I was able to reflect and re-focus my heart and life. Through homesickness and loneliness, I learned to throw myself deeper into the arms of God. In heartbreak, I learned

---

7 Romans 8:28.

8 "An Interview with the Writer, Speaker, Artist, and Former Oil Executive: Luci Swindoll." Interview by Nancy Lovell. The High Calling. July 4, 2006. http://www.thehighcalling.org/articles/essay/interview-writer-speaker-artist-and-former-oil-executive-luci-swindoll.

to better care for others. Disappointments of this life showed me glimpses of heaven waiting in the next.

A flame in the night is never extinguished by the darkness. On the contrary, the darkness defines the flame's outline all the more. Suffering has a purpose — to work for and reveal good. That revelation of good may come about in others. It may come about in us. It may be instantaneous, or it may be in the future. It may be to reveal a glimpse of the glory of Almighty God Himself. Our choice is whether we will let suffering break us to bits or break us down just enough that God can build us up to be even stronger than we were before.

This is often easier said than done. Maybe you are nursing a child with a rare form of brain cancer and can't understand what kind of God would let this happen. Perhaps you long for a child to fill your empty nursery, but you still don't have one. Maybe you just buried your beloved wife, and your heart feels smashed to pieces. Or perhaps your husband has chosen someone else and left you alone, ashamed of his bad choices and abandoned with more responsibilities than you ever expected.

Where's God now? Do you want to trust a God who would let this happen to you? It seems cruel. You don't want to know your pain has a purpose. You just want the pain to stop.

The only way that I could release the pain from my heart was to take it to my compassionate, Almighty God. Remember how Jesus wept at the grave of Lazarus, the man in the Bible who was raised from the dead? Jesus knew His friend would walk out of that tomb, but He still wept because He loved his friends.

He loves us, too.

He doesn't do things randomly or by mistake. He is a "man of sorrows," the Bible says, "acquainted with grief." He is a God who can "sympathize with our weaknesses" (Isa. 53:3, Heb. 4:15 NASB). He didn't go through this life unscathed either. He came down here, put on the same kind of skin we wear, and suffered for us.

I have watched my precious sons encounter heartbreak and sickness on the mission field. But God's son died for us here.

I said goodbye to things I loved. Jesus left the beauty of heaven for me.

I have been betrayed and wounded. Jesus was sold by a "friend" and then was mocked, spit at, beaten beyond recognition, and killed. He didn't give Himself a free pass in this department. He could have, but He didn't.

He hurt for us. He still does.

I've had many, many opportunities to look back and see that the hand of God brought good from my hurts. Sometimes, the miracles were obvious; other times, they were worked out privately in my own heart and soul. I've seen Him send a small trial to prepare us for a bigger one, and I've also experienced trials that were designed to move me to a place where I could comfort someone else who was hurting.

Though I don't always want to admit it, God occasionally uses challenging circumstances to rub off my rough edges and make me more compassionate. Sometimes, my heartache teaches me something I need desperately to learn. And I believe that, other times, our trials exist solely to draw us closer to our Creator.

What about the times when I can't see those answers and don't know the purpose of the pain? I need to rest in the knowledge that He has been faithful in so much already. When I glance back at our stacks of stones, showing His work in our lives, I can trust Him for the things that I don't yet understand. It's not an easy solution, but it is real. I have to surrender my own ideas about what should be done and believe Him.

Of course, that takes intentional steps day after day. In times of suffering, I prayed, read the Bible (especially the Psalms), and sang songs of hope and joy — even when my heart didn't feel very gleeful. I chose to claim that His joy was indeed my strength.[9]

I went to church too. Psalm 73 gives a long list of injustices and then says, "It was too painful for me — Until I went into the sanctuary of God" (Ps. 73:16b-17a NKJV). I love that. To spend time with hopeful, Bible-believing Christians, instead of staying home locked in despair, is an important step. Speaking and singing

9 Nehemiah 8:10

words of hope, instead of spewing out complaints and demands, is another.

We have the power to choose.

One of my heroes is Joni Eareckson Tada. After a diving accident in 1967, seventeen-year-old Joni became a quadriplegic. After much grappling with God, however, she chose to live life fully — even with enormous challenges and struggles. She became an internationally known speaker, author, musician, artist, radio personality, and advocate for the disabled, as well as the founder and CEO of Joni and Friends International Disability Center.

Joni says that our suffering is like a match, with great potential for good or for harm. It can be used to start a ravaging forest fire or grill a steak for dinner. We can make a choice what to do with the mighty power of that flame.[10]

During some of my hardest days, when daily tasks seemed unbearable, I would do what she says she has done many mornings. Before getting out of bed — even before opening my eyes sometimes — I would tell God that I didn't have the strength to handle what was ahead. I needed Him. I needed His strength. I echoed Joni's prayer: "I have no resources for this. I have no strength for this — but You do."[11] And day after day, He provided me with everything I needed to rise and face the trials and triumphs that lay in front of me.

I survived the sadness of abuses, illnesses, poverty, and corruption in Bolivia the same way I survive the sadness of deceit, divorces, apathy, addiction, and despair here in America — by leaning on Jesus and not on my own understanding. It's not denial — I feel the pain too — but I believe He loves me and has a plan for me even in the midst of suffering.

Years before we ever arrived in Bolivia, our older son, Peter — who was then about two years old — got very sick with a virus. Unable to keep even water down his throat for more than fifteen

---

10 Eareckson Tada, Joni. "Chapel: Joni Eareckson Tada, Jan. 14, 2013." Address, Westmont College Chapel, Westmont College, Santa Barbara, CA, 45:19. January 14, 2013. https://www.youtube.com/watch?v=c3Q0FkVPs04.

11 Tada, Joni Eareckson. *Hope: The Best of Things*. Wheaton, IL: Crossway, 2008. Print.

minutes, he was running a high fever and becoming dehydrated. We couldn't get the situation under control. So we called his doctor and made the thirty-minute drive to the hospital. Once there, they evaluated him and almost immediately began to prep our precious little boy for an intravenous line.

Our son is very logical, and was so even at that age. He couldn't understand the logic of strangers poking needles into his arm when he already didn't feel well. He began to call upon my husband for help.

"Daddy, please make them stop! They are hurting me! Please, Daddy!"

Tom's heart was breaking. This was our firstborn child. We would have died for him. He was so little and seemed so helpless. We were supposed to protect him.

How Tom wanted to stop the pain for his scared and hurting son! But the intravenous fluids were crucial, and Tom knew that.

"I can't," he choked out. "I know it hurts, but you need this to get well. They are trying to make you feel better."

We realized an important truth by watching our little boy that day. After he heard that message from his daddy, whom he trusted, he stopped struggling. Then those big blue eyes looked up at the nurse as she pierced his baby skin and drove a needle into his tiny arm. "Thank you," he said bravely.

She began to well up too. "Don't thank me!" she answered.

But his response was correct because he knew something I hadn't yet learned. When the Father you know is trustworthy sends pain that you don't understand, you can rely on Him and lean into it. You can even be grateful. Our Father God sees the whole picture when we can't. He knows that sometimes suffering is for our own good — to save us from a riotous crowd on a train trestle, to rescue our bodies from fever, to keep us from relationships that are dangerous, to lead us away from jobs that would suffocate our passions.

We usually want the path of least resistance, but it's often through the hard that we find the best.

If you are faced with suffering this week, be strong and

courageous. Hang on. Face it squarely — even with gratitude and thanksgiving. God is there with you, has suffered for you, and loves you more than you know.

"Not only that, but we rejoice in our sufferings, knowing that suffering produces endurance, and endurance produces character, and character produces hope, and hope does not put us to shame, because God's love has been poured into our hearts through the Holy Spirit who has been given to us" (Rom. 5:3-5 ESV).

Bolivian women from the highlands often carried their babies in brightly colored woven blankets, worn as slings on their backs.

BROKEN

By Janine

I don't know where to turn sometimes —
I don't know where to start.
It seems that everywhere I look,
there's more to break my heart.

You are the God who sees me, Lord,
wherever I may be.
You know the hurt that's in my soul,
You see the suffering.

I bundle up these cares I have —
the wounds this world bestows —
and lay them at my Father's feet,
this weight He can dispose.

With burdens resting now on Him,
weight shed, I still will weep.
My heart still breaks for what breaks His.
My Father's love's so deep.

TOM AND JANINE THROSSEL

We cry together at the place
knowledge and caring meet,
and I find peace and promise there —
hope at my Healer's feet.

CHAPTER SEVEN

RESPONSIBILITY: OUR ROLE IN SUFFERING

By Janine

I ASSURE YOU, I DIDN'T CRY.

Not when my friend gave me the news so brusquely that I doubted her Christian charity. Not when my son came to fetch me, and we waved goodbye. Not when I settled in beside my husband and rode the few blocks to the gas station.

I didn't.

While I waited for our tank to fill with diesel, however, something snapped. Heavy, throaty sobs came from deep within me, and Tom was at my side in an instant, asking what was wrong. Tears drenched my cheeks, hands, and clothes. I knew I was scaring my family, but I had reached the limit of restraint.

I finally managed to groan that I was fine, but that I had received some bad news about Paola. I didn't tell them what it was, though. How could I tell my little boys the rumor I had heard — that their 13-year-old friend was "working" at a bar in the seediest section of the city? They knew she had run away. They knew she had been hurt. Did they need to know this new information too?

I had fought hard to save her. For years, I had counseled, advised, pleaded, prayed, and begged for her. When there were marks on her body, I took her into my home for the few hours I was allowed. When there were marks on her heart, I took her to a youth camp and out for pizza. I brought a social worker to talk to her family. I held out hope and offered solutions. Yet the government was not on my side. Most of her family was not on my side. Even her church was not on my side. She had to stay where she was. I hadn't known what else to do.

I suspected that the stresses were breaking Paola down. I wasn't completely surprised when she ran away. But this? My soul bore a terrible weight that spilled over into weeping. And I knew that, no matter how deeply I suffered, that little girl was suffering more.

It's an ages-old question: *Why, God?*

Where are You in the midst of this? Do You care? Do You hear us? Why don't You stop this pain? The queries are echoed in enough books to fill library shelves.

As I wrote in the last chapter, I understand that my sufferings have brought me closer to God, have been for my good, and have been for the good of others. I believe that, through everything, I am very blessed. I have come to accept so much comfort from God and to trust Him for the answers I don't know and through the pain I don't understand in my own life.

But what about Paola? How did the sins against her work for her good? What about so many others like her? I grew tired of hearing stories of child after child hurt in such seemingly indelible ways. Though I am but a vapor on this earth, with no right to ask Him, I, too, have risen up like so many others to ask God, "Why? Where were You?"

I can't say anything on these pages that will make Paola's suffering seem okay or justifiable. I think that's as it should be. Her situation isn't okay. There is, I believe, a God-given longing within us for justice, goodness, and wholeness. I didn't see justice come to Paola. The way she was treated by most of her family left her broken and battered — body and soul.

Yet there is something I need to say — with all due respect and humility — about this kind of suffering. It sometimes exists because we the church are not doing all we should do.

We are quick to blame God for the world's sorrow when He has already told us how to help solve so much of it. He has told us how to love people and invest in their well-being. He has told us to show compassion. We ask God to end poverty, but we don't give. We ask God to help people in far-off places, but are we willing to be the ones to go and reach them? He has provided a way of rescue for some of the world's suffering, and some of that plan is supposed to involve us.

In this generation, we often joke about "first-world" problems — internet that isn't fast enough, two television programs scheduled at the same time and no way to record them, the price of gasoline for the cars we drive a few blocks because we don't feel like walking. I confess I do it too. But very real problems in the third-world country where I lived — problems like Paola's — caused me to reflect much more seriously on suffering. It caused me to ask some very hard questions.

Questions like these: How much suffering is not caused by coincidences or the normal valleys of life, but by wrongdoing? By people hurting other people? What are we supposed to do about that? How are we equipped to bear some of this burden?

What about the concept of ending poverty? Is it feasible? Are we responsible for any of that? Could we actually manage our money in a way that would alter our world?

Questions beg for answers, and I didn't have all the answers I wanted. So, I did some digging. And what I found is a little hard to take.

Did you know that the average person's weekly budget here in America includes $14.40 a week for coffee-shop drinks,[12] $7.82 for tobacco, $6.67 for cable TV, $3.68 for amusement parks, $4.83 for jewelry and at least $8.05 for liquor?[13] Those six luxuries alone run more than $45 per week. Yet most people give less than $10 per week to physically fight problems like human trafficking and

12 News, ABC. "How Much Does the Average American Spend at Coffee Shops Each Week?" ABC News. August 06, 2012. http://abcnews.go.com/GMA/american-coffee-habits-spend-coffee/story?id=16923079.

13 "Consumer Spending Statistics." Statistic Brain. October 15, 2015. http://www.statisticbrain.com/what-consumers-spend-each-month/.

to provide resources like orphan care and clean water. In fact, a significant percentage of us give less than $2 per week.[14]

Barna research reveals that evangelical, churchgoing Christians are the most giving group in the USA when it comes to charity. Almost all church-attending evangelicals donate *something*, whether that is money, items, or time. They also tend to give in more generous amounts than many other groups. I was glad to see that Christians do lead by example in this way.[15] Yet few of them give the 10 percent tithe we read about in the Bible. In fact, a recent report said churchgoers average a "tithe" closer to 2 percent, and most of them give less than that.[16] I wonder what this world might look like if Christians gave five times what they give now!

And time? Did you know that Americans watch an average of almost thirty-two hours of television per week? Or that they spend about thirty-five hours a week on mobile devices doing things like playing video games and using social media?[17] What if we spent even a couple of those hours doing something else, like volunteering or praying for someone in need?

We all have busy schedules and need time to rest, rebuild and relax. Also, some screen time actually can be legitimate and purposeful.

We all have expenses, too. Finances can get painfully tight. I'm not suggesting that we shouldn't ever use our money or time to benefit ourselves.

Yet I wonder sometimes why we blame God for problems that we could really help solve.

When we look at the magnitude of evil around us, we can be tempted to grumble, grow weary, and lose faith. But God always gives us a way of escape from temptation; we don't have to fall

---

14 Group, Barna. "American Donor Trends." Barna. June 02, 2013. https://www.barna.org/barna-update/culture/606-american-donor-trends#.VzeDDuTQPIA.

15 Ibid.

16 Briggs, David. "The Flesh Is Weak: Churchgoers Give Far Less Than They Think." The Huffington Post. September 1, 2012. http://www.huffingtonpost.com/david-briggs/the-flesh-is-weak-churchgoers-give-far-less-than-they-think_b_1846516.html.

17 Kleinman, Alexis. "Americans Will Spend More Time On Digital Devices Than Watching TV This Year: Research." The Huffington Post. August 1, 2013. http://www.huffingtonpost.com/2013/08/01/tv-digital-devices_n_3691196.html.

into it. Sometimes, that way to peace is through simple trust in a magnificent God. Sometimes, however, He calls us to action.

For example, we don't just will away an addiction or a bad dating relationship. We have to get up and walk away. Seek counsel. Get help. We have to act.

It's the same with our relation to the problems of the world at large. God doesn't leave us to despair. He gave us a job to do. It isn't enough to sit and blame God. The longer I know Him, the more I see that He has given His children wisdom and strength beyond their comprehension to help others in His name. So, why don't some of us do it?

As I searched for answers and read statistics, I was reminded of some of the amazing men and women who contributed to our work in Bolivia. I thought about one woman who told us that she hadn't thought that she could afford to help. Then she realized that she was spending a lot of money at a particular coffee shop and decided to send it to us instead. She cut out those frequent visits and sent us fifty dollars a month, helping us literally to feed the poor and bring relief and hope to the needy. I think of a boy who sent me a handful of dimes from selling chicken eggs. I think of an elderly man, sending one dollar a month, his thin, drifting handwriting telling us he was praying for us every single day.

Let's be honest: For some of us, a couple of dollars a month still seems like a big sacrifice. But every gift is significant. God has promised that if we give our tithes to Him, He will make our money stretch,[18] and we saw He was faithful over and over again to make that happen. Those people gave what they could, and God blessed and multiplied it.

We ask, "Who is going to do something about rescuing children, drilling wells, feeding the starving, and fighting AIDS?" Let us never be people who expect a solution without being willing to sacrifice anything ourselves.

Are we going to dare to do nothing and then ask God why He doesn't do more? Why don't we do more with all He has

---

18 c.f. Proverbs 3:9-10, Malachi 3:10, Luke 6:38, Proverbs 19:17, Matthew 6:31-33.

abundantly given us? If we don't, how can we be surprised each time evil wins?

Does it feel overwhelming? I think of Elijah in the wilderness,[19] feeling so discouraged and alone. The odds appeared to be so greatly against him — and against righteousness. But God had seven thousand people waiting in the wings to help. Elijah was never truly alone. With God on His side, he was far from hopeless or helpless.

Our family has met and partnered with some amazing people on this journey. People who have spent money and sent workers around the world. Some have helped rescue women from brothels. Some have fed individuals who were homeless. Some have provided after-school care for at-risk children. Churches we work with have helped to fund wonderful outreaches in Africa, Europe, North America, South America, and Asia.

By contrast, Paola's church didn't give her the support and protection she needed. The members were good at so many other things, yet they failed her in that. Looking back, I sometimes wonder if I failed too. I tried to get her help through the government, my own efforts, friends, her family, and youth care homes. I hinted to people in her church, but I didn't push them hard enough to make the abuses stop. They had connections in the community. They had the power and Spirit of God. They might have changed the trajectory of her life. I don't say that to blame or shame them, but to challenge us.

Where was God? He was loving Paola and grieving over her while His church — the people that He told to defend the fatherless and protect the innocent — didn't do all that He commanded. Would we have?

I learned something else I want to share about these kinds of struggles. Certainly, there will be times that, despite our strongest efforts, it will seem we are unable — at least temporarily — to turn the tide. So while we are praying and advocating as best as we can, there is something else we can do.

A North American counselor of rescued children came to visit our team during this difficult season with Paola, and I asked him

---

19 I Kings 19

for some advice about this precious girl. "I can't get her out," I explained. "I can't get her to a shelter. I can't take her to the police for help. Right now, those aren't practical options. What can I do to help her?"

His guidance was simple: I should be an example for her and provide a safe place for her to rest. So, for her and for others, my family and I began to do that. I couldn't take all these children's problems away. I couldn't control what happened in their homes or neighborhoods. I couldn't change the laws in a country that wasn't my own. But we could model for these children the kind of homes and families they could create someday when they were on their own. We could try to show them God's love. Together with my family and teammates, I could provide a place – however temporary – where no one would ever intentionally hurt them. We could teach them how to search their Bibles and how to ask God for help and comfort. We could provide a brief respite away from the pain and sorrow. We could tell them about safe homes that were willing to take them if they could get their freedom. We could prepare them to leave their past in the past as soon as possible and move ahead into the future.

These may seem like tiny, insignificant actions, but as famed basketball coach John Wooden used to say, we shouldn't let what we can't do keep us from doing what we can. It's like those single dollar bills wrapped in a widower's letters and prayers each month – It all adds up. Sometimes, we can't rescue people from their situations, but we can point them in the direction of hope. And that makes a huge difference.

I wish I could say that there has been a fairytale ending for Paola. I wish I could say she is healed of her heartaches. I wish she was in school, in church, in a family that lavished love on her and saw it reciprocated. In reality, there have been a few highs and some deep lows.

She did return briefly. By this time, after all she'd been through, she was considered by family and government to be a lost cause. So we were able to take her to a care home without permission from her relatives.

However, she was unable to process the quiet life and lack of drama in her new home, and she returned to her family. Surrounded by evil once more, she eventually left them again. One of her abusers died shortly afterward and, though I pitied him, I couldn't find it in my soul to weep for him.

I last saw Paola at a wedding. She was smiling, but smug. Her hair was dyed, her makeup was thick, her clothes were tight. She was fifteen. Later, someone told me she was pregnant, but I never saw a baby.

A short time later, another one of her relatives died. I went to the cemetery, hugged family members, listened to the sermon, and watched the casket drop into place. I hoped to see Paola there. I wanted another chance to talk to her. But she had refused to attend the service, and I stood at the grave, wishing.

Janine loved spending time with girls at a care home for abused and abandoned children. The two little sisters grinning at the camera were brought in with health issues that included malnutrition and head lice, which is why their heads were shaved. Their mother, battling AIDS, was too sick to care for them on her own.

RESOURCES

Are you interested in giving more of your own time, money, or talents to make a difference and help others? If so, we recommend that you check out these organizations. One may be a good fit for you!

Compassion International — *Releasing children from poverty in Jesus' name. Compassion works around the world, with an emphasis on child sponsorship.*

Compassion International
Colorado Springs, CO 80997
(800) 336-7676
http://www.compassion.com

International Justice Mission — *Working with local authorities in developing countries to rescue victims, bring criminals to justice, restore survivors, and strengthen justice systems. IJM fights human-rights abuses that include slavery and human trafficking.*

International Justice Mission
PO Box 58147
Washington, DC 20037
(703) 465-5495
http://www.ijm.org

Joni and Friends — *Accelerating Christian ministry in the disability community. This organization reaches out in numerous ways, including teaching how to better serve disabled people, giving wheelchairs away, providing family retreats, and hosting relevant radio and television programs.*

Joni and Friends
International Disability Center
PO Box 3333
Agoura Hills, CA 91376-3333
(818) 707-5664 or TTY: (818) 707-9707
http://www.joniandfriends.org/

SAMAIR Bolivia — *A ministry close to our hearts, they are providing safe, reliable air transportation for church associations and missions in Bolivia. Christ's love is demonstrated through service to communities by meeting medical, social, spiritual, and physical needs.*

SAMAIR Bolivia
c/o South America Mission, Inc.
1021 Maxwell Mill Road, Suite B
Fort Mill, SC 29708
(803) 802-8580
http://www.southamericamission.org/

Samaritan's Purse — *Following the example of Christ by helping those in need and proclaiming the hope of the Gospel. Samaritan's Purse has ministered around the world for more than thirty years, through earthquakes, hurricanes, wars, and famine.*

Samaritan's Purse
P.O. Box 3000
Boone, NC 28607
(828) 262-1980
http://www.samaritanspurse.org

Teen Challenge USA — *Teen Challenge offers a Christ-centered, faith-based solution to youth, adults, and families who struggle with life-controlling problems such as drug and alcohol addiction.*

Teen Challenge USA
5250 N Towne Center Dr
Ozark, Missouri 65721
(417) 581-2181 or 855-ADDICTION
http://www.teenchallengeusa.com/

CHAPTER EIGHT

ENCOURAGEMENT: WORKING
AMONG THE AYOREO

By Janine

*"Enga Dupade chijnorapise erámi jogosórone ore. Jecute
tẽra dajnacare ugurui ome ore. Ujetiga gosi changureta
enga gajneque pucuecaringué eyúgojmai iji deréjnane jnese.
Enga a ca chimo Dupade ujuyaquedatei jne ome re."*

— John 3:16 in the language of the Ayoreo people[20]

I F I WERE TAKING YOU with me to an Ayoreo encampment, we
might jostle over bumpy roads along the outskirts of a city
to a squatter's camp or fly in a small airplane to a village
with thatched roofs and a concrete slab for soccer. The youngsters
probably would come to meet us either way, jumping onto the
outside of someone's truck without asking, their bare feet gripping
hold and their brown-and-orange-streaked hair drifting in the
wind. Adults would gape and giggle unabashedly. Many people
would be missing teeth, and a few would be missing various
clothing articles we might find important. Most would be carrying
handicrafts woven of coarse plant fibers or whittled from wood —
bows and arrows, sculptures and carvings, necklaces and purses.

---

20 Misión Nuevas Tribus, Cochabamba, Bolivia. "San Juan 3:16." In *The Ayore Bible*. Faith
Comes By Hearing. 1982. http://www.bible.is/AYONTM/John/3/D.

Some of those would be for their own use, but many would be for sale, if the money was right.

The Ayoreo are a lowland tribe, one of at least thirty-five Bolivian ethnic groups with indigenous heritage. Their first language is not Spanish, but Zamucoan—a staccato, nasally voice heard by very few other people in this modern world. There are fewer than 6,000 Ayoreo left, according to statistics.[21] Once a warrior nation of nomadic people, they have been forced to adjust to their neighbors pushing in from all sides. No longer can they strip the land where they are and move on to take from the field next door, because "next door" is often property that legally belongs to someone else. The Ayoreo may be strong enough to stop other men, but they're not strong enough to stop those men's guns, laws, or jails.

Their story of contact with the modern world has been sad at times. Seventy-five years ago, their immune systems were not ready to fend off the colds, flu, and other diseases that some eventually caught from meeting their neighbors. Simple illnesses swept through Ayoreo families like the plague, racking up fatalities. Their cultural beliefs about land ownership also led to violent confrontations that killed some of them as well as some of the strangers they approached. As farmers and ranchers basically bought ground out from under them, the Ayoreo fell from self-sustaining to impoverished. Suddenly, the mighty hunters had nowhere to hunt. How could they possibly understand this shift of fortunes?

They lost respect, as well. "Civilization" wasn't ready for the unique tribe's companionship. To this day, when Ayoreo come to look for work or receive medical care in the city, they are often ostracized, marginalized, and treated with contempt—if they are treated at all. They have had little voice among their fellow countrymen and often resort to begging and prostitution for income.

Some experts believe that the Ayoreo should be allowed to live uncontacted by modern society, as they lived for generations. But

21 Infantas, Anna. "Bolivia's Ayoreo Indians, Devoured by the City." Inter Press Service. December 18, 2012. http://www.ipsnews.net/2012/12/bolivias-ayoreo-indians-devoured-by-the-city/.

it's too late, and their little corner of the world is too crowded. The department of Santa Cruz, where many from this tribe live, has doubled in size in twenty years and now holds more than two million people. Who is going to move away, and to where? The Ayoreo have reached out to the world as much as the world has reached out to them.

With this history, and with groundwork laid by other missionaries decades before, a tiny team from South America Mission (SAM) works to meet some of the needs of the Ayoreo just as they are, in their current context. To live in the modern world, the tribe has to understand more of it. Hardworking friends of ours teach the villagers hygiene to fend off disease, agricultural techniques to supplement their diets, finance and economics so they receive fair wages for their handicrafts, and cultural norms so they can receive better treatment in big towns and cities.

The Ayoreo also need to have a voice. So these missionaries encourage them in the establishment of government structures that give their people political influence in their country.

SAM workers have helped meet physical needs, buying them land to live on, farm, and hunt—something the Ayoreo could not yet provide for themselves. They established a medical clinic for them when society around them refused to touch or treat them. These missionaries perform surgeries, deliver babies, treat diseases, and counsel emotional needs—often for no charge. They emphatically warn girls away from prostitution but are still willing to treat their wounds and show them compassion. The missionaries don't ridicule the Ayoreo's cultural norm of leaving young children to fend for themselves, but they helped establish a center where those kids can wander safely and receive food and an early start education in their own language. The SAM missionaries give generously of their time to these amazing people and love them in culturally relevant ways—instead of just talking about what should be done.

In the midst of this delicate balance of joining the ancient and modern world while preserving cultural integrity of both, outsiders are sure to notice some entertaining differences. We don't completely understand, for instance, the way tribe members laugh when someone is hurt or falls down. We didn't expect tribal children to show up at a pool naked when they were invited to come swimming. Tom cringed to see revered elderly women tearing apart a tortoise roasted at a meal in their honor. I have often wondered how the tribespeople live so comfortably with so much dirt on their skin.

There have been plenty of moments of laughter as our cultures collided, such as when someone proved the strength of an arrow by shooting it into a couch, when a girl flooded a bathroom by trying to wet her hair under the sink's faucet, and when tribal women chased a pet parrot to pull feathers off for their artwork. Likewise, they are amused by us—the way we talk, the way we dress, the way we eat, the way we act. As "normal" as we think we are, we are mutually entertaining!

Ayoreo church services are different from those of my childhood as well. For instance, Ayoreo meetings can easily last three hours. If an American church service lasted that long, we might look at our watches and sigh in irritation, but the Ayoreo don't wear watches. Their buildings are intentionally different, too. To reflect the nature of the group, one building I worked in was round, not rectangular, with a hole at the top to let out wood smoke from a central fire.

There also is a great cacophony of sound in the church. The Ayoreo do not conduct their meetings in the formal, scheduled way that many Americans do. Church gatherings are much more conversational. The sermon is discussed among the audience members—while it is still being given, and sometimes in multiple languages. This kind of commotion can be quite unsettling to a newcomer.

During our years in Bolivia, I had the great privilege to work often with Ayoreo children. Sometimes, it was difficult for me to focus on what I was trying to tell them—in Spanish—while they discussed it with each other in a blend of Spanish and Zamucoan. It was hard to tell if they were listening at all or just talking among themselves.

One day, I was asked if I would travel to an Ayoreo village and care for the children during a women's conference, when their mothers would be too busy to watch them. I was excited to spend a day with this group of children from different settlements. But my usual teaching teammates were all busy. Tom also planned to be about 650 miles away, visiting church leaders in El Alto with Philip. I was grateful when Peter — who was a freshman in high school — enthusiastically agreed to be my assistant, and two Bolivian friends who were unfamiliar with the tribe agreed to help with games between my lessons. I was responsible for planning about six hours of teaching and activities.

In the weeks before the conference, I spent a lot of time praying, studying, and praying some more. The Ayoreo culture is a storytelling one, and they love to hear stories from the Bible. I knew early on that I wanted to teach from the lives of different biblical characters, but which ones? Peter? Daniel? Elijah? David? One by one, the stories came together. One troubled me, though. I had a clear sense that I needed to teach a lesson about Stephen, but that story presents a bit of a challenge. In fact, it's the kind of story that I think a lot of Sunday school teachers skip altogether.

Most of the others are stories of victory. Peter believed God, and an angel broke him out of prison. Daniel believed God, and God closed the mouths of lions that would have torn him to pieces. Elijah trusted God, and instead of death, he left for heaven in a chariot of fire. David trusted God, and he defeated a threatening giant. Who doesn't want to hear stories like those?

Some of Stephen's story, though, is quite sad and seems very unfair. When Stephen talked about Jesus Christ, the religious leaders of the day got angry at him and threw rocks at him until he died. This is not exactly G-rated material. But I really thought that I was supposed to share his story with the Ayoreo kids. I didn't know why, but it gnawed at me every day as I prepared.

It's difficult to explain why God allowed Stephen's death and why it's important. It's hard enough for adults to understand, not to mention children who speak the same language as the teacher. The Ayoreo kids and I had a language barrier and a cultural barrier.

On top of that, as I said, it is normal for them to walk around and chatter during the lessons. How could I explain this story to them without creating more questions than I was answering?

It didn't make sense to me, but I knew God wanted me to do this. So I studied, planned, and prepared. We had a suitcase of props, and Peter was going to act out some of the characters while I narrated. We planned to do some singing, tell one of the stories, do a craft project that matched the story, and play some games. Then we would repeat the process—singing, story, craft, games—four more times. We would have occasional snacks as well, including small fish-shaped crackers that American friends had donated as a gift. (Unaccustomed to the shape and flavor of one of our favorite treats, the Ayoreo children later said the crackers must be vitamins. North Americans were always bringing them vitamins!)

The day arrived. It was early March, the end of their summer. We began to set up in the only space appropriate and available to us. In the middle of the mud huts and rough concrete buildings, there was a paved slab that served as a place to play volleyball. The Ayoreo children sat down there in a large circle, while Peter and I, with my notes and our suitcase of props, stood in the center. To include all of the children, I walked around as I spoke. I asked questions, shouting so that they could all hear me over the constant noise of their own discussions. Some of them were translating to those near them, transforming my Spanish words into the Zamucoan equivalents. Some seemed to be discussing what they were hearing. Others just seemed to be talking about what to do with the rest of their day. As the time passed, about sixty children came and went, the crowd swelling and shrinking with restlessness, the bright heat of the day, and the smell of food in the distance.

I wondered if we were keeping their attention, but when I asked questions about the stories, they were quick to respond. When we got to game time, they wouldn't line up to play. They usually love games, so I didn't understand until one of them told me, "We don't want to play games. We want to hear more stories!"

I was happy to oblige them.

A fight broke out at one point in the lessons, with two of the children scrapping and throwing punches in the middle of the circle. This, too, is common in the culture, and even as my hands reached out to pull the boys apart, I kept teaching — in an even-louder voice.

How could I possibly teach them the story of Stephen in a way they would understand, in the middle of all this chaos?

Peter and I had prayed for them to understand, and I had to trust God that they would. So, as the day got hotter, and the sun sank lower, I launched into this final story. I told them about how Stephen loved and believed God, but the local religious leaders were mad at him. He was willing to contradict them publicly when they were wrong, and they didn't like that. Members of one group talked others into spreading lies about him and stirring up people against him.

Stephen was innocent. All he was doing was telling the truth, yet they kept after him. When the high priest in the high council asked him if the lies they were telling were true, it was a tricky question to answer. Would he call them out as the schemers or liars they were? He answered by taking them back to school, telling them highlights of their own history. He spoke in detail about past events and how time after time the religious leaders actually stood against God's ways instead of with them. He told them that they were doing just what their ancestors did — resisting God!

They didn't take kindly to that. The Bible says they gnashed their teeth, covered their ears, and yelled at the top of their voices. But Stephen was given the opportunity to see heaven open and see Jesus standing there. The leaders dragged Stephen out of the city and began to stone him, to pummel him with rocks that would eventually kill him. Stephen prayed, "Lord Jesus, receive my Spirit!" and "Lord, do not hold this sin against them!" Then, he was in the presence of God (Acts 7:59, 60 NASB).

I told the children that, in the other stories, we saw God answer the way we wanted Him to answer. In the story of Stephen, however, we saw Him answer in a different way. Maybe we would have preferred for Him to save or avenge Stephen. Instead, He lovingly takes Stephen to heaven. We might see that as sad or bad, but what we don't realize sometimes is that He knows what is best. In many situations, He rescues us. But in many others, He doesn't save us — at least not right away. In this case, the very best move was to take Stephen to the splendor of his everlasting life, not to keep him in the earthly life where he was.

After hours of wiggling, talking, giggling, wandering, translating and poking at each other, I expected the children to continue to behave that way. I figured I would have to keep talking loudly. But as I got to the end of this story and shared these deep spiritual truths, the children were silent.

I don't know if I had ever heard them silent in nine years of working with them. When I asked them questions about what I had just said, they gave correct answers. We talked about what the story meant, and they prayed with me.

I have taught hundreds of Bible lessons to many different children — rich ones and poor ones, children from different races and tribes and families. I hope that I never forget that hot March day with those children on that wide concrete slab.

Sometimes, God does things the whole world finds remarkable. Other times, He works in less noticeable ways. Sixty Ayoreo children silent during a Bible lesson? Choosing Bible stories in the sun over running games in the shade? I might have believed I could walk on water before a little miracle like that would happen. Yet those kids needed to hear that lesson, I needed to teach it... and God worked out the details.

Typical Ayoreo houses in the Department of Santa Cruz were built with mud and sticks.

In an Ayoreo church building, Tom and other volunteers showed children how to create art from items around them, including sticks, leaves, and flowers.

ECCLESIASTES

By Janine

I
T WAS A LOVELY DAY *for a church service. Warm, as usual. City buses rolled over the paved streets, picking up and dropping off passengers. A horse-drawn cart moved slowly down the intersecting dirt roads, and a vendor called out from it, selling fresh fruit. Dust rose and fell in the air, settling onto recently washed faces and once-clean church clothes.*

Inside our stuffy little classroom, about twenty children sat on the wooden benches that lined the walls. Kids from two to six years old hopped in and out of those seats, like popcorn popping on a skillet. None could read yet.

Each week, I was privileged to teach them great stories from the Bible. I told them about the prophet Daniel, King David, Noah and his boat, and the strongman Samson. The kids and I sang, snacked, and played games together, and I awarded stickers when they learned their weekly Bible verses.

Then, as class was ending, we would enter the room where the adults sat, and we would say together as a class: "Buenos dias, hermanos y hermanas. Les saludamos en el amor del Señor. (*Good day, brothers and sisters. We greet you in the love of the Lord.*)"

"Amen!" *the adults would exclaim. The children's salutation was a longstanding tradition, and parents would beam with pride when their well-behaved boys and girls executed it properly. Then we would recite the verse of the week, sometimes showing our artwork or singing a song or two.*

This particular day, the children were fairly quiet and attentive during their class time. I squatted in front of them so I would be closer to their height. I was teaching them from the third chapter of Ecclesiastes.

The familiar words, "For everything there is a season, and a time for every purpose under the heaven," often are attributed to Pete Seeger and The Byrds, but their original source is the Bible. It is Ecclesiastes that says:

> *a time to be born, and a time to die;*
> *a time to plant, and a time to pluck up that which is planted;*
> *a time to kill, and a time to heal;*
> *a time to break down, and a time to build up;*
> *a time to weep, and a time to laugh;*
> *a time to mourn, and a time to dance;*
> *a time to cast away stones, and a time to gather stones together;*
> *a time to embrace, and a time to refrain from embracing;*
> *a time to get, and a time to lose;*
> *a time to keep, and a time to cast away;*
> *a time to rend, and a time to sew;*
> *a time to keep silence, and a time to speak;*
> *a time to love, and a time to hate;*
> *a time of war, and a time of peace. (KJV)*

As the class ended, I was talking to the children about emotions and asking them questions based on the fourth verse in this passage.

"When do you feel happy?" I inquired. "When do you want to laugh?"

They responded much as I expected they would, with little-kid answers about being with friends and running fast. Then I asked them the question that would stay with me for years to come.

"When do you feel sad?"

I had expected answers like these: When I don't get what I want in the marketplace. When I have to turn off the lights and go to bed at night. When my mom doesn't let me have any candy. When I don't get to do what I want.

Those weren't the answers I got, though.

"When my mommy beats me," one child said.

"When my dad left," another added.

My heart caught in my throat, and I blinked back tears. The majority of these children were just four or five years old.

I wrapped up our talk, and we went to recite our memory verse to the adults. But I couldn't stop thinking about those children and the heartaches that they had already experienced, even before they reached kindergarten.

The class that day reminded me that we all have stories.

In the years that followed, I did my best to remember that fact each and every time I taught a class, no matter the age or subject matter. School or church, English literature or Spanish grammar, Bible class or history class — each child and each moment I spent with them was valuable and precious.

Some of those children didn't get breakfast that day. They witnessed fights in their families that morning or saw their moms crying. Some of them woke up without a parent in the house at all; all they had was a neighbor to walk them to the church. They didn't get the hugs, cookies, and bedtime stories that we did as children. Just being present in class that day was a huge accomplishment for some of them.

In the years that followed, we would begin to work in another community where children would walk miles alone just to go to church, leaving their parents unconscious in the town courtyard from drinking the night before. Those children didn't come for treats and fancy famous speakers. We didn't even have a building to meet in, just a spot in someone's yard. They came to hear about Jesus, because deep in their hearts, they knew He was real and life was meant to be different, better.

Seeing the perseverance and passion of all these children changed me. On that day with my class studying Ecclesiastes 3, and in the days to come as well, I did my best to make my classes worth their effort. I tried to remember to invest in each of them, to give them my kind and full attention, to teach things that mattered.

Teaching is a privilege that shouldn't be taken lightly. Teachers have the incredible opportunity to give an important gift — a time for children to heal, to laugh, to dance, to speak, and to love.

CHAPTER NINE

CITIZENSHIP: TIMES OF LAMENTATION

By Tom

GROWING UP IN NORTHERN CALIFORNIA, I hadn't witnessed much racism. I heard about race riots and studied Rosa Parks in school, but I never saw much of it firsthand. By our second term in Bolivia, however, we were quite aware of racism, and it was not always directed toward us.

Yes, we had been charged "gringo prices" for market items and taxi rides – taken advantage of because of our skin color. We'd been stopped by the police for no legitimate reason. But what we saw happen among the nationals was much worse.

The Andes mountain range runs down the western side of Bolivia, effectively dividing the country into two sections. On one side are the dry, cold highlands. The air there is thin enough to induce nosebleeds and even heart attacks in visiting tourists. Citizens dress in traditional fiber clothing, and many also are traditionalists politically. It is a land of llamas, salt flats, potatoes, and reed boats, with a reputation for strong, resilient people.

On the other side lie the eastern lowlands. It is hot there, with plenty of rain and vegetation. The land is fertile and yields produce a lot easier than in the west. The bustling city of Santa Cruz de la Sierra is renown for flowering trees and for the cassava root that is served as a delicacy. People there – businessmen with international interests or parents who send their children to learn English, for example — tend to be more globally minded.

Sadly, the people known as Paceños, who live in the rugged highland mountains, are often hated by the Cruceños, who live in the eastern portion of the country. And the hatred goes both ways; some of the Paceños speak just as intensely against the Cruceños.

Many highlanders had moved to the city of Santa Cruz where we lived and had integrated into the way of life there. But division persisted. Our church often had both groups worshiping together, which was somewhat uncommon, and they worked as a team. Yet, on rare occasions, we still heard a degrading comment from one side or the other, even at church.

To add gasoline to this already heated relationship, Bolivia's first elected highland indigenous president was quite outspoken in favor of his own people. Nursing the hurts from a history of frustration and inequality, he and his followers played more and more political games to punish the Cruceños for what he considered disrespect of him and his people.

Race riots broke out throughout the country in 2008. Large crowds of people formed in the highlands and started long marches toward our city for the purpose of teaching the lowlanders a lesson on respect and strength. Armed with sticks, rocks, and guns, the marchers seemed to grow more and more violent as they got closer to us. Some of the lowlanders who went to speak with them on the road were assaulted and sent home. Lowlanders still in the city began to boast of the thrashing they would give the highlanders when they finally arrived at the town plaza.

As the tension grew and some talked of civil war, many foreign humanitarian groups pulled their people out of the country. Even the American embassy closed its doors, after US Ambassador Philip Goldberg was ejected and declared a persona non grata by President Evo Morales.

As Janine mentioned in an earlier chapter, we were given the option of heading home to the States until the situation settled down. But we were confident in our mission leaders and in God's ability to protect us. Bolivian friends on both sides of the debate told us that if things got ugly we could go to them for safety as well.

It was during this tense time that I received a phone call from Miguel.

Miguel was a youth who had grown up in the church that my family had begun to attend. He had become a good friend of mine. He often helped with whatever projects Janine and I were working on, and he regularly called me just to talk. His love of soccer and music were only overshadowed by his love of his family and God.

Miguel's family came from the highlands, but he had spent almost his whole life living in a small barrio of lowland Santa Cruz. His mother wore traditional clothing and kept her hair in two long braids down her back, typical of the highland women. She also cooked some of the best highland food I've tasted. Miguel's sister, on the other hand, wore modern, western-style clothing. She had loose, flowing hair and played sports like her brother.

Miguel's call that day surprised me, because he said he wanted to talk face to face. That sounded serious. I had received similar calls from other members of the church's youth group, and they usually had one of two things to say: "I have a financial need, and I'm wondering if you can help me," or "My girlfriend and I are expecting a baby and getting married, and we want to invite you to the wedding." I hoped Miguel was not calling for either of those two things.

When he came to the house, we picked up a few bottles of Coca-Cola and headed to a quiet spot along the canal to chat.

Miguel didn't need money, and he wasn't starting a family anytime soon. He wanted to talk because he felt as if he were being pulled apart. His family and heritage made him empathize with the highlanders, even as his friends from church, school and the neighborhood were siding with the lowlanders. He was seeing people on both sides being killed on television. People pulled at him to choose a side. He saw the country he loved and the people he loved being violent toward each other, and he didn't know what to do.

He wanted me, a neutral outsider, to help him choose.

"Who is right?" he asked. "If my country goes into a civil war, who do I fight for?"

Before I answered, I remembered what the Bolivian president had warned the *extranjeros* (outsiders or foreigners). He basically had told us all, "You have no political voice here. You are invited guests, and your visa into our country can and will be revoked if you publicly take a political stance."

I saw good and bad on both sides. Who would *I* have fought for? They both had points that I understood and agreed with, yet both sides had stepped over the line into violence and rage. More than thirty people were dead, including one pastor who was shot while holding his Bible, trying to mediate between the factions.[22]

I wasn't sure how to answer Miguel's questions.

Then the Israelites came to mind. I thought of how they had built up Jerusalem and the temple, only to have it destroyed while most of them were taken away into captivity by the Babylonians. What would that have felt like?

The Bible describes it this way in the book of Lamentations:

> I have cried until the tears no longer come;
> my heart is broken.
> My spirit is poured out in agony
> as I see the desperate plight of my people...
>
> Peace has been stripped away,
> and I have forgotten what prosperity is.
> I cry out, "My splendor is gone!
> Everything I had hoped for from the Lord is lost!"
>
> The thought of my suffering and homelessness
> is bitter beyond words.
> I will never forget this awful time,
> as I grieve over my loss. (Lam. 2:11, 3:17-20, New
> Living Translation)

Don't those words sound like they could have been coming from Miguel? His city wasn't demolished, and his family hadn't

---

22 Pastor Luis Rivero was shot on September 12, 2008.

been carried off into captivity. But he could understand some of the heartache. Peace, prosperity, and splendor were gone. The mighty warriors were weakened, starved, and captured. The people were weeping, not celebrating. The familiar had been lost, and the future looked scary. Bolivia wasn't a pile of rubble and desolation like Jerusalem was, but many of the feelings were still the same. Miguel wasn't looking back at what had happened, but he was looking ahead at what might happen. He was still grieving, bewildered, troubled, and sad. Maybe even a bit afraid.

Miguel, like the Israelites, was in a very tight spot.

But their stories weren't finished yet. In the third chapter of Lamentations, there is a verse that changes everything.

"But this I call to mind and therefore I have hope" (Lam. 3:21 ESV).

Like those stones that we talked about so many chapters ago, the Israelites could recall something that gave them hope. Their past experiences and knowledge of God added stability and assurance to their rock pile.

> The steadfast love of the Lord never ceases;
> His mercies never come to an end;
> they are new every morning;
> great is Your faithfulness.
>
> "The Lord is my portion," says my soul,
> "therefore I will hope in Him."
>
> The Lord is good to those who wait for Him,
> to the soul who seeks Him. (Lam. 3:22-25)

The Israelites were in captivity, and their city was destroyed. But God was still in control of their world, and they knew it. At the height of their turmoil and heartbreak, God was still capable and good.

Bolivia also was facing the threat of war, and the situation looked dire. But God was still in control. He was still good to those who waited for Him and sought Him, those who didn't lean on their own strength and understanding, but on His.

That afternoon, as we walked along the canal, I did my best to tell Miguel that God was more concerned with his heavenly citizenship than He was of his earthly citizenship. No matter what happened in the days to come, God was in control. Even if a civil war ripped his country in half, even if people died — no matter what, God could still take care of him. If he didn't fit on the highland side or the lowland side, he still fit on God's side.

This truth doesn't make everything easy, but it does make survival possible. It makes hope, peace, and even joy possible.

In those days of destruction back in Israel, there were people who stood firmly in the midst of it all, trusting God. The prophet Jeremiah saw the needs of his people and bravely spoke up. Shadrach, Meshach, Abednego, and Daniel were young Jewish captives. Yet despite their youth, they lived without compromise, even when threatened with death (and God saved them). Nehemiah, a Jewish cupbearer to the Persian king, would see the grief and destruction of his people, and he would raise up an army to rebuild the city walls.

Miguel would have to be like them and trust God, no matter what happened.

He lived up to the challenge. He simultaneously stood by his family and his friends, while remaining true to God's calling on his life.

As the swelling, angry mob approached our city, it was hard to imagine a happy ending to the conflict. Peace seemed like wishful thinking. Talks were failing, and angry people joined forces — not just a few fringe extremists, but truckloads of strong, passionate men and women. We were warned to stay away.

Then Christians started assembling to pray for peace. They didn't just pray quietly in their hearts and homes. Individuals, neighbors, and numerous churches gathered in public places to pray. For the first time in Bolivia, I saw Catholics praying together with evangelical Protestants. Instead of adding to the violence, much of Santa Cruz de la Sierra stopped and prayed.

And as that fierce, armed mob got closer and closer to the city, its marchers slowly and surprisingly stopped.

After weeks of traveling from the dizzying mountain altitude of more than 10,000 feet to the muggy lowland weather of Santa Cruz de la Sierra, they just quit. Some of them began to fight among themselves and ceased fighting together for their cause. Some of them apparently grew tired—just an hour or two's drive away from their goal. Someone speculated that perhaps one of their leaders quietly called them off.

What I know is this: For weeks, the highlanders marched toward the city with a message of hate, fear, and pride. Hate, fear, and pride came from lowlanders too, as they prepared to fight back. But in the end, other lowlanders chose love. And perfect love casts out fear. The highlanders couldn't stand and fight while drenched in the prayers of God's people.

*A nighttime view of the city cathedral in the
Plaza 24 de Septiembre was magical.*

City buses lined up in traffic outside a market known as La Feria.

PARCHED

By Janine

Composed during crop burning season

The pale earth outside my windows has been scorched dry

by hot winds and a baking sun.
Smoke sullies the air and, when I step into the thick haze,

thorns stab like spears into my bare feet.
The weight of it all presses down hard, heavy, into my soul.
It is not just the land here, but people who are parched and depleted.

A girl just into her adulthood, holds her wide-eyed son.
She is thin. Frightfully thin.

She tells me another baby — a girl this time — is on the way.
I gasp before catching myself. "Next week?"
I see the tiny bump in her belly and swollen gums in her toothy smile.
"I didn't know you were pregnant," I stammer.
"Neither did I," she answers.
And she sells me chocolates — two for a quarter — and tells her quiet boy

they will soon buy something to eat.
He never makes a fuss.

A friend speaks of two more girls shattered, wrecked, betrayed,

by someone who should have known better.
Lord, come quickly.

We are weary, wilted and withering.
How do we find justice in an arid place? This desert space?

Yellow grass struggles to hold on;
rusty blades have already succumbed.
The sand is hot,
not just thirsty, but empty.

The sky is thick with rain, but it isn't falling.
And I look at the brown, curled leaves that

used to frame delicate flowers.
I see the dusty sticks in dead soil,
and I wonder if, down below the gray, hungry surface,

the plants still have life in them.
Somewhere, way down deep — beneath, beyond, below —

are there bits of green?
Cells still working?
Resting maybe?
Gathering hope and strength for another day —

A day when God will bring them out anew?

My own soul feels detached.

Surrounded by pain, I struggle to see the life that is still in me.
The presence of the Vine wrapping around

my own stubbornly-still branches.
Yet "I remain confident of this:
I will see the goodness of the Lord
in the land of the living." (Psalm 27:13 NIV)

We ache for the rain. The scent of it on choking land.
And then, we pray for it.

Why does that so often come as an afterthought?
We ask and our Heavenly Father, in His unequaled mercy,
sends us what we long for. Not just drops, but showers.

Streams, flooding down from the rooftops, filling up

the empty places, soaking, soothing, slaking.
He bathes His children in glimpses of His glory.

Lightning, bright and beautiful, flashes in the distance.
I lie in bed and hear the thunder.

I wonder still – will it be enough this time?
Oh, dear Father, help my crazy unbelief.
You are always enough.

Lord willing, a young woman will come to visit tomorrow,
to talk of English and Spanish, and hopefully God.
And this weekend, my house will be filled with teenaged moms –
among them, one with bleeding gums and a wide-eyed little boy.
And I will serve them something to fill their bellies,
and hopefully, something to quench their spirit's thirst.

"Wait for the Lord;
be strong and take heart
and wait for the Lord." (Ps 27:14 NIV)

CHAPTER TEN

RELATIONSHIP: A TRIO OF TORTOISE TALES

By Janine

Part One: Drinking Deep

L IVING IN A FOREIGN COUNTRY can mean a new interpretation of the word *pets*. In North America, we had goldfish. In South America, friends kept parrots, tarantulas, monkeys, and even a toucan. We did get more fish in our new home, as well as some guard dogs. We also ended up with some surprising and delightful additions to our family — five *Chelonoidis carbonarias*, our red-footed tortoises.

Torta la Tortuga came first, as part of a house we rented. Our landlady asked if we would mind caring for him — making sure he had water to drink during the dry season and an occasional banana or bit of salad. It didn't take long for me to fall for the critter (and then fall over him, as he would fix himself underfoot like a boulder). The landlady eventually gave him to us. He was very spirited and would chase us — Tom especially — around the yard. He would pace back and forth to get our attention, stare down our German shepherd until the poor thing whimpered in fright, and eat food from a fork in my hand. Torta was hilarious.

Ronnie came next. Born at a friend's house just before Christmas, he was given to Tom as a gift. Ronnie was so cute and small compared to Torta.

Our mama tortoise came to live with us a few days later. Friends working in a village rescued her from a near-certain future as food. At Tom's request, they brought her to the city for my birthday. Her shell was scratched and scarred, but we called her Bella, or "beautiful." It took some time for Bella to stop hissing at me and adjust to her life with us. But bit by bit, she learned we were safe and would take care of her.

Finally, after Torta and Bella had been acquainted for about a year, two little tortoises were born in our back yard. We called them Tortilla (a spin off from Torta la Tortuga) and Sherman (because he was built like the tank).

Tortoises are natural scavengers. Since they had less hunting and roaming space with us than they would have had in the wild, we supplemented their diet, provided water, and modified their living arrangements a little bit. But they aren't high-maintenance animals. While water turtles have very specific needs, raising red-footed tortoises was simple in lowland Bolivia. They ate a lot of vegetation, bugs, and carrion, and they burrowed in the dirt to sleep.

They drank from puddles, which I would sometimes create with the garden hose in drier seasons. One day, I took the time not only to make sure puddles existed in the yard for Torta, but also to watch him for a while as he drank. The sight cut me to the quick because that critter was all in. He didn't just lap at the water's edge. He submerged his leathery little head into that mud, and his neck expanded and collapsed with gulp after gulp of life-giving liquid. It didn't matter that he couldn't see what he was doing. It didn't matter that he was getting dirty and mucky. It didn't matter that the puddle would be there all day, and he could have come back later and gotten a little bit more. While it was in front of him, he was going to ignore everything else around him and drink all that he could. And, at the risk of sounding too philosophical, it made me think.

I remembered another story about Israelites. This group lived about three thousand years ago and got a reputation for drinking deep. The book of Judges tells that a group of Midianites was persecuting and impoverishing them, destroying their crops and ravaging their land. The Israelites cried out to God for help, and He sent a prophet to tell them what was happening.

God had already delivered the Israelites from a different enemy—the Egyptians—who had enslaved them. After that, He had given them land to live on, which they shared with a group of people called the Amorites. He had told these precious Israelites, people who He obviously loved and cared about, not to worship the false gods of the Amorite nation while they lived there. But they did anyway. So He sent Midian to teach them a lesson and get their eyes back on Him. The Midianites harassed them so badly that the Israelites moved into forts, caves, and the clefts of the mountains. Yet they still wouldn't listen to God or ask Him for help. For seven years, they tried to win their own way.

Finally, in desperation they cried out to Him. It was a tough-love lesson, but it worked. Their eyes were finally back where they needed to be. God told one Israelite man named Gideon that now they could attack Midian and drive them back.

But Gideon was scared. He saw himself as weak and incapable of leading an army against this mighty throng of threatening warriors.

It was hard to see at first that God didn't want them to attack in their own strength. The point was for God to show them His own might, glory, and care for them. He wanted them to learn to trust Him and depend on Him. Many things happened to Gideon as he fought through the idea that God really wanted him to lead a battle against the Midianites, and that God, not the Israelites, would win it for them.

During this process, God helped Gideon prepare his army. Gideon had 32,000 men standing with him. But since this was about God's strength, not Gideon's, God told Gideon that he had too many men. Too many soldiers? Whoever heard of that? God had a plan though. He told Gideon to announce that anyone trembling with fear could leave. After seven years of bullying by the Midianites, there were plenty of trembling soldiers. Twenty-two thousand men left the group. Gideon was down to 10,000.

But God wasn't done yet. He instructed Gideon to take them to the water so He could thin out the army further. I can't even imagine what was going through Gideon's mind at the time. He had witnessed the tactics of the Midianites. His army had already been cut down by more than two-thirds. And yet God said that was still too many men?

God led them down to the spring to drink, and what happened next is what reminded me of our tortoise. Nine thousand seven hundred men drank like Torta—faces in the water, slurping with abandon. Three hundred men scooped water with their hands, then raised it to their mouths and lapped like dogs. And those 300 were the soldiers God chose.

The 9,700 men who plunged their faces in the water were submerged in trouble. With disaster around them, while their nation was hoping for their protection, they were focused on themselves. Only the 300 laid their own wants aside so they could keep their heads up. This showed they could diligently fulfill the responsibility they had been given.

I thought about that story after I saw my tortoise drink so freely from that puddle. There is something within us that drives us to be all in, isn't there—a desire to plunge our heads in without looking around and drink with abandon? That's not a bad thing in itself. It can even be admirable. But it's what we are drinking from that matters. In Lewis Carroll's story *Alice in Wonderland*, Alice said that she didn't much care where she was going, so long as she got somewhere. That attitude is a recipe for disaster. This world is full of poisons and remedies. What we drink from makes a big difference.

I want to go in the right direction. I want to drink deep from the fountain that saves me from this world and from myself. I want to drink deep while God's goodness is in front of me, not waiting to come back some other time. I want to plunge myself beneath the spring of His grace and not come up for air until He has filled me with His peace and abundant life. He is, as He said centuries ago, living water that will completely satisfy us.

After Gideon had narrowed down his group of soldiers to 300

men, God told him to go to the Midianite camp and eavesdrop. When he got there, he found the enemy's camp contained so many Midianites, Amalekites, and other eastern nationalities that he couldn't count their camels any better than he could count the sand on the seashore. But he also overheard someone in that giant crowd telling of a dream God had sent to him — that the Israelites would destroy Midian. God had told His enemies that they were going to lose!

Encouraged, Gideon took his 300 men to the hilltops. When their trumpets sounded, God took charge. The Midianites turned against each other, and the battle was miraculously won.

Gideon's tiny army didn't choose to drink of fear like the first 22,000 prospective soldiers or self-servitude like the next 9,700. They drank deeply of God's promises, obedience, and trust. And they were rewarded for their faith.

Oh, the joy there is in drinking deeply from the fountain of salvation! [23]

Part Two: Turtles in Training

One day, one of our tortoises had a medical emergency that required treatment. I went online to look for tips on tortoise care, and as I perused articles and comments about repugnant ailments like shell rot and malnutrition, something caught my attention.

It was a picture of a box turtle that had been found in the woods and had become a family pet. I imagined a young boy's excitement that first day when his parents let him keep the creature. How impressive the terrarium must have looked after they prepared it for him — sparkling glass sides and a floor of smooth, polished rocks.

I thought of the home our tortoise Ronnie lived in. He wasn't big enough to be let loose in our big yard yet, so we had made him a sort of den too. It was a large plastic washtub filled with a little bit of dirt. The red basin was dull and scratched. I don't think any of us would have called it polished or sparkling.

23 c.f. Isaiah 12:3 NLT.

Every so often, I would carry it outside, lift Ronnie out and transfer him to another safe place, and unceremoniously dump the grimy muck from the bottom of the tub into the grass. I would add fresh soil and drop in handfuls of leaves, flowers, and other plant material from our lawn. If one of my sons or I had a little extra time and inclination, we would make designs with the flowers, leaves, and rocks—just to give Ronnie a little change of scenery. A big piece of broken pottery formed a cave for him. A giant rock gave him a climbing goal that he could never quite master. His water dish was constantly walked across, burrowed under, and flipped upside down when he was bored.

This little pen made up most of his world as he knew it. We would take him out and let him walk on the actual earth from time to time. Most often, though, he roamed around in his simply furnished home, which was, I suppose, quite similar to the ground outside. It was nothing fancy.

At times, I felt a bit sorry for him. He didn't have much to keep him busy or to make his habitat look pretty.

But then I saw Prince, the little box turtle.

I imagine that Prince's owners had great intentions as they cared for him. They must have loved him to want to keep and raise him. But when they put him in that lovely-looking terrarium, they didn't realize how his environment would hurt him.

Prince was badly deformed, with little legs that were bowed and bent, and it was all because of those rounded stones and that shiny glass. He couldn't dig his toes into terra firma or burrow down deep in it to hide from the cold. He couldn't stretch to climb a giant mountain of a rock when the surfaces his feet rested on were so slick and smooth. He was made for dirt, not beautiful rocks. He was made for the flat and boring, not the bumpy and glossy. His little legs couldn't negotiate the gravel. His slipping and sliding and lack of opportunity to stretch his legs and walk "full speed" caused permanent, horrible damage to them. It made me so sad to see pain in his present and limitations in his future because someone unwittingly tried to keep him in a setting where he wasn't meant to be.

How I wished sometimes that my life looked pretty from the outside—like Prince's terrarium with its glittering transparency and shine. I wanted other people to find my life and home to be serene and refined. I wanted it to be easy and comfortable. I wanted my office to be orderly. I wanted to do mighty things—at no cost to me. I desired to accomplish all my goals with a perfectly clean house, stunning meals on the table, no sleep deprivation, and no fights with anyone—myself included.

But God knows better than that. So He makes things a little tougher, a little rougher, and a little more like the coarse terrain He knows is up ahead for me. He builds my muscles. I have to dig in, push, climb, and struggle. I strain the way that Ronnie strains for the hundredth time to climb a rock he is not yet ready to climb. But one day, Ronnie will be big enough, old enough, wise enough—and he will be ready.

May I be ready too, dear Lord. May I learn to savor the struggle so that my legs will be firm and my heart will be brave and sure.

Part Three: Listening to That Still, Small Voice

"After he has gathered his own flock, he walks ahead of them, and they follow him because they know his voice. They won't follow a stranger; they will run from him because they don't know his voice."

(John 10:4-5 NLT).

Our adult tortoises, Torta and Bella, were finally parents. Tom found their first tiny offspring near their nest, with its shell still soft and leathery. We were thrilled beyond words. What an incredible thing to see!

We brought that newly-born tortoise into the house to protect it from the many dangers of our yard and set up a new pen near Ronnie's. One-year-old Ronnie had grown to about the size of a small bagel by then, while the baby's diameter was about that of a Ritz cracker!

One typically sultry morning, I realized that Ronnie and the baby — Tortilla — had been cooped up inside for about twenty-four hours. The afternoon ahead looked promising. I expected a few sprinkles, but no serious rain. I thought some fresh air and even a faint little shower would be good for the creatures in such hot weather. So I brought their portable plastic containers outside.

I placed Tortilla's washtub on a table inside the carport, sheltered under a roof. He could feel the breezes but stay protected from rain, sun, and birds. Ronnie, however, had been outside often. I decided to put him on his normal perch, a low, wide brick ledge among some tall, potted plants. He would have sunshine, sky, and perhaps some leaves to reach for above his little head. It was a much more natural environment and view than the one Tortilla had.

As I left him there, though, I felt an odd tug in my heart. It was an unmistakable pull to take him from where he was and move him over to the covered table. But that didn't make sense. He would be so much happier on the ledge!

Tug.

Was it unsafe? I didn't think so. He had his little cave to hide in, in case a bird came around. He even had a heavy rock to weigh the tub down so it wouldn't blow over in the wind.

I ignored the tug and left him on the ledge.

Although Ronnie had spent a couple of nights outside in clear weather, Tortilla had not. I fully intended to bring them back in after an hour or two, but I forgot. I was in the middle of doing the evening's laundry when I first saw lightning — a flicker in the distance so faint that I thought a neighbor's light bulb was going out. Then it came again and again.

The tortoises never crossed my mind.

It was late, and my family was already asleep. I lay down too, and as the raindrops began to splash, I looked forward to a good night's sleep. I love the rain and the gentle way it breaks the heat and falls like a summer lullaby. Within minutes, though, the rain had turned into a huge storm. The lightning was blinding and the thunder was intense enough to wake my husband. Flashes and booms came almost exactly together. And there was so much water! Bucketfuls poured from above, flooding our lawn.

Summer storms can come and go incredibly fast in that part of the world. It hadn't been long—perhaps five minutes—since the rain had begun in earnest. But as the noise became more intense, I got up to make sure the children were sleeping well and that our computer was unplugged in case of a lightning strike.

Tug.

The tortoises!

I ran to the door. Before we moved into this rental, someone had installed four locks on the front door to provide security from robbers. How I wished that weren't the case as I fought to get outside to Ronnie. I fumbled with the keys. Finally, I stepped across the wet and filthy patio floor to find Ronnie's head and the top of his shell bobbing at the surface of about two gallons of water. He was a land tortoise, and he was fighting for his life, bouncing off his climbing rock to gulp air and not fall to the bottom.

My heart sank, soared, and pounded all at the same time. I plunged both hands into the muddy water and scooped him out, rushing him to the still-dry dirt of the baby tortoise's pen.

I carried that pen and its occupants inside the house. I was amazed as water continued to pour from inside Ronnie's shell—I have no idea how it could hold so much. I lifted him out and warmed him between my hands, then wrapped him in a towel to dry him off some more. Eventually, he curled up among some grass and leaves in a corner of the baby's home and went to sleep. He woke up the next day fine and seemingly content.

I know I could have killed him that night.

God doesn't often send us messages that boom like thunder. He doesn't often write boldly on a wall or in the clouds. He usually speaks more softly than that. But He does speak to our hearts. As we walk with Him, we learn to recognize His voice. We know when it's God talking and not our own fanciful thinking.

He is so personal that, at times, He speaks about something as minor as two pet tortoises. Other times, the subject matter is far more important. It concerns our jobs. Our habits. Addictions. Relationships. And we know we've heard from Him.

Even then, though, we sometimes struggle. *That can't be God's voice*, we think, *because I don't agree with it!*

But we know. We can fight all we want, but we know.

And He knows something we don't. He knows what is ahead. He knows that to give up a bit of sunshine overhead today may save us from dying in a flood tonight. He knows.

"Oh, for grace to trust Him more."[24]

---

24 Stead, Louisa M.R.. "'Tis So Sweet to Trust in Jesus." Lyrics published in 1882. Copyright: Public Domain.

Our tortoises were such a source of delight! In addition to Tom's tortoise, the brave swimmer Ronnie, we had our comic relief, Torta (left), and our challenging girl, Bella (right). Torta and Bella eventually had two babies, Tortilla and Sherman.

TIRED FEET

By Janine
for Jenny and Katie

Awkwardly, I slide my dusty feet
Beneath — far beneath! — my plastic chair
Callused heels, stained by pock-marked streets —
Dirty feet, not soft nor fair.
Evening soccer and ironwood trees
Falls bruise and break us as we run this race.
God sees our feet so differently
He, who brought us to this place.

Isaiah, His prophet, wrote long ago:

How beautiful on the mountains
are the feet of those who bring good news,
who proclaim peace,
who bring good tidings,
who proclaim salvation,
who say to Zion,
"Your God reigns!"[25]

---

25 Isaiah 52:7 (NIV)

Jesus walked on this planet, same as we —
King's feet, sandaled, stepping into the vile.
Love drove Him from manger to temple to tree,
marked those feet with nail holes of self-denial.

No guilt for a salon day with my sisters
Or scrubbing off the grime for soft pink lacquer
Painted swirls, though, or humble blisters —
Quicken our steps, God, to go where life matters.

Restore our passion, our perspectives renew
Strengthen our hearts to live Your love here.
Teach us bravery as we look up to You.
Untie the laces that have bound us in fear.

Vibrant and vital, we want to run strong.
Wrest away doubts that hold us back
X-ray us, show lies we've held too long.
You alone can fill our every lack.

Zealously, joyfully, we sprint forward — even with tired feet.

CHAPTER ELEVEN

TRUTH: LET'S BE HONEST

By Janine

E ACH OCTOBER, OUR CHILDREN'S MINISTRY Team worked with a local church that encouraged children to deepen their love and awareness for people around the world. Organizers would assign our team the names of foreign countries, and we would teach spiritual lessons based on those places. We talked about the power of prayer in Afghanistan, fighting fear in Somalia, and the life of Hudson Taylor in China. As the years went by, our adventures also took us on imaginary trips to India and the Philippines.

I dug deep each year, reading and researching, shopping and creating. Some years, I even cooked traditional foods like lumpia, tea eggs, and tandoori chicken for my family as I tried to increase my understanding of the cultures we studied.

My teammates were great. From wearing a sari, burqua, or pith helmet to leading interviews and trivia contests; from singing in Swahili to making international flags out of colored paper, each one gave in abundance of their time and talents. It was always a highlight of my year.

Once, our assignment included Burkina Faso. I hadn't known the tiny, land-locked country in western Africa even existed until then. It didn't receive its independence from France until 1960, and has only been known by its current name since 1984. It's a nation that's barely older than I am!

Burkina Faso is about the size of Colorado. However, instead of tall, snowy mountains and five million people in that space, imagine dry, dusty African flatlands and more than 16 million people.

As I began to research Burkina Faso, what I found at first seemed lovely. The Internet and travel guides spoke of a place that was captivating and enchanting, full of cultural distinctions and exotic beauty. One personal blog I read described Burkina Faso as a kind of utopia, unhindered by the modern mayhem we experience in the West. Though the country is largely Muslim, it appeared to be characterized by religious freedom and a lack of divisiveness. Muslims, Animists, and Christians seemed to live in relative quiet and coexistence.

The more I researched, however, the more I found a dark and disturbing side to the nation. Many teenage girls there face illegal forced marriages, polygamous husbands, and domestic abuse. If they refuse to marry or are childless, they face serious stigma from their community.[26] Most children are allowed to spend only eight years in school, especially if they are females. The majority of the population still cannot read or write. Approximately 77 percent are unemployed. As was true in Bolivia, children younger than ten risk their lives slipping into shaky underground tunnels to mine treasure for other people's pockets.[27]

The health situation sounded dire as well. The life expectancy for people in Burkina Faso is less than fifty-five years. They are subject to numerous infectious diseases and more than a quarter of the children are considered underweight. Their AIDS infection rate is nearly double ours in the United States. Their infant

---

26 Brady, Martha, Lydia Saloucou, and Erica Chong. "III.The Social and Economic Context of Girls' Lives." In *Girls' Adolescence in Burkina Faso: A Pivot Point for Social Change*, 7-9. Ouagadougou, Burkina Faso: Population Council, 2007. http://www.popcouncil.org/uploads/pdfs/BurkinaFaso_Girls.pdf.

27 Price, Larry C. "Burkina Faso: Childhoods Lost in the Gold Mines." Pulitzer Center. April 28, 2013. http://pulitzercenter.org/reporting/gold-mining-child-labor-burkina-faso-kollo-ILO-labor-rights-commodities.

mortality rate is ninth highest in the world. There is approximately one doctor for every 20,000 people.[28]

Perhaps they didn't have the hassles of gridlock, materialism, and computer crashes that we have here in the West, but they certainly had some issues of their own.

As I continued to prepare for the conference, I discovered one more interesting tidbit about the country of Burkina Faso. I learned that masks play an integral role in Burkinabe society, both culturally and spiritually. These masks aren't simple, domino-style coverings like those of Zorro or the Lone Ranger. They are time-consuming works of art, skillfully carved from the wood of the silk-cotton tree. They are not fashioned from a set of printed patterns, either, but from the images in the artists' brains, described and handed down through generations.

A typical finished work is made from one single board and can reach six feet in length and up to fifty pounds in weight. Imagine the strength that the person wearing that mask must have as he balances that load with just a stick crossbar held between his teeth!

These carved masks often are painted in striking geometric designs, with colors coming directly from the earth: tar from the seed pods of Acacia trees, dark powdered charcoal, bright chalk, clay, the red dust of stones dense with iron, and sun-lizard dung. Additional adornments include honey, mud, chewed kola nuts, cowrie shells, porcupine quills, horns, tusks, seeds, beads, and even animal or human blood or excrement.[29]

Sometimes entire body costumes are created. Plant fibers are soaked in mud, beaten, knotted, twisted, and occasionally dyed. Then they are attached to a net foundation and draped over a man. When completed, a masked dancer resembles a spectacular monster.

Visitors to Burkina Faso may see the swirling, colorful displays of this mask dance tradition, and think of it as innocent fun. But the masks aren't just heirloom art or an attraction for tourists.

28 "The World Factbook, Africa: Burkina Faso." Central Intelligence Agency. May 6, 2016. https://www.cia.gov/library/publications/the-world-factbook/geos/uv.html.

29 "Burkina Faso's Case by Case." African Art Museum. 2013. http://smafathers.org/museum/burkina faso from oaoo i to v/.

They are created to contain and invoke spirits, receive the blood of animal sacrifices, guard traditional secrets, remind the people of religious laws and stories, protect families and fruit harvests, escort the dead to the afterlife, and bring gifts — such as children, work, money, and rain.[30] The masks are a serious business.

As I sewed a facsimile of an African dress and made a (non-traditional) papier-mâché mask to show the children at the conference, I began to think about the way masks hide the true image of the person underneath. I don't believe that Burkina Faso, as a nation, is intentionally hiding its "other face" — the great needs and fears of the people there. I do, however, think that we sometimes see only what we want to see. At times, we look at something alluring, like the peaceful outside image of Burkina, and then close our eyes to whatever may lie behind that.

That illusion of peace reminds me of a couple of experiences I had in Bolivia.

One night, I hired a taxi driver to take me to a particular grocery store I liked and then return me home. I could have taken the *micro* — a bus about the size of a minivan. I was going alone, though, and it was hard to maneuver bags of groceries on and off a crowded bus. Besides, this was a taxi driver Tom knew, and he was willing to wait the short time I expected to spend in the market.

I was walking the store aisles contentedly when the overhead lights went out. They came back on after about three seconds and people resumed their shopping. But I began to notice a few unusual things. I saw some employees whispering to each other. One of the two front doors was pulled shut. A man positioned himself by the remaining door, cheerily funneling customers through it after they completed their purchases.

My family and I once had been in a very large marketplace in Costa Rica where a power failure led to a panic among the crowd on the inside. That was not an experience I wanted to repeat. So, spurred by that memory and the unusual behavior of some of

30 Roy, Christopher D. "The Art of Burkina Faso." Art and Life in Africa. Accessed May 15, 2016. https://africa.uima.uiowa.edu/topic-essays/show/37?start=3.

these store employees, I quickly got into a line with my groceries and checked out.

When I exited the building, I stepped into a much different world. Inside the store, it was bright, cheery, and calm. Outside, the dark night wrapped around flashing caution lights, emergency vehicles (which we hardly ever saw in Bolivia), and a crowd of hundreds of people. My taxi driver, who was standing nervously outside his car, jumped toward me as I walked into the fiasco.

"I was about to come get you," he exclaimed. "I didn't know what to do!"

You see, the side of the store was on fire!

I went home, stunned. While the store employees were positioning themselves near the exits, encouraging customers to shop and taking the money we gave them, the store was literally burning. They made us think it was safe inside, masking the danger. Our ignorance wasn't bliss; it could have killed us.

It wasn't true peace, just an illusion of peace.

I experienced this frustration again — and much more so — on a very hot day in November. It was that day, with the tropical sun melting me into the pavement, that I met two sisters, whom I will call Fernanda and Eva.

These girls had been through a lot of heartbreak. When they were four and seven years old, they had witnessed the death of their mother at the hands of her abusive boyfriend. They then lived four years with their biological father, who beat his girlfriend. One day, after the girlfriend left, he gave his daughters about seven dollars and told them he was going to travel for a few days. Then he disappeared.

Two months later, a neighbor saw the girls climbing trees in search of fruit. The neighbor contacted their cousin, Maria, who was a live-in maid miles away in the city. Maria quickly traveled out to the countryside to get Fernanda and Eva, and moved them into her very small bedroom in her employer's house. But after about a month of keeping them there, the employer said the girls could not stay any longer.

No other family members were reliable or wanted the

responsibility of caring for the girls. So Maria sadly returned them to their house in the country and began traveling there weekly on the bus, checking on them and bringing them food.

It became too much for her to handle. She was a college student, with a big job and a small paycheck. She could have quit school and worked more hours. But as one of nine children, with her own set of irresponsible parents, she was trying to provide financially for her brothers and sisters and break the cycle of sloth and poverty in which she was raised. The situation with her little cousins was eroding her—emotionally and financially.

She wanted Fernanda and Eva to have schooling, food, and a safe place to live. She said she would work hard to set all this up for them, to be able to take them in a year's time. But she wasn't quite ready yet.

So she brought them to me, hoping I could place them in a good home for the next twelve months. I called a Bolivian social worker I trusted to help us through the government process.

One of the first things the social worker told Maria was that she needed to stay behind as we entered the government offices. She warned that her presence could complicate the case. Yet Maria refused to send Fernanda and Eva unaccompanied, and after all that had happened, I could hardly blame her.

We all paraded into the Bolivian equivalent of the Department of Children and Family Services—the social worker, the cousin, the sisters, and me. Despite one of the girls being quite ill and in need of attention, and despite our having a list of two government-approved care homes and two private homes all willing to take the children that day, we were denied.

As the social worker had predicted, the government official did not consider these girls to be in enough crisis to override their father's custodial rights. It didn't matter that he had been gone for four months by then, without a word. Maria was present and obviously concerned for them, so she was expected to take them in or immediately return them to their father's little house in the country. She was not to place the girls outside of the family. She was to wait for the dad's return, continuing to check on them and bring them food. The official didn't say where the coins for groceries and bus fare should come from. Fernanda and Eva, ages eleven and eight, weren't in need, apparently. They were "just fine." Case closed.

Before I said goodbye, I spent some time talking to them. We made sure the sick girl received medicine, and we told Maria to call if there were more problems. We told her about the homes—including my own—willing to take the girls if she could talk a court official into surrendering their guardianship. To go against the court would mean criminal kidnapping charges for her or for us.

And I talked to all three of them about hope and the power of God. The girls had already suffered so much, and their situation looked bleak. But I told them the truth—that with God, all things are possible. The girls could have a future and hope in Him. God could redeem them. I have watched Him transform lives, and I believe it with all my heart. It was not too late for them. Yet, oh, how it hurt to say goodbye that day and wonder what paths they would have to take before they got to that future.

The situation didn't feel just fine. It felt like another case of saying "peace, peace" when there was no peace.

This sort of masked truth is nothing new. In approximately 600 B.C., the "Weeping Prophet" Jeremiah preached about this very thing. He kept telling the nation of Israel that they were headed for disaster, capture, famine, and exile. But a group of false prophets told the people not to listen, that they would be just fine. They didn't want to make waves and rock the national boat.

So the people mocked Jeremiah and kept doing what they were doing. No matter what he told them, they refused to act on it, even to save their lives.

God said of the false prophets: "They have healed the wound of my people lightly, saying, 'Peace, peace,' when there is no peace" (Jer. 6:14, 8:11 ESV).

Sure enough, what Jeremiah predicted came true. A siege led to extreme famine. The city was captured and burned, and citizens who survived all of that were exiled to a foreign land. On that sad day, the false prophets were surrounded by the evidence that Jeremiah had been telling the truth. The people weren't just fine.

Just saying there is peace doesn't make it so.

Recently, I heard an archived recording of an esteemed psychology professor from an Ivy League school. He remarked that we "are probably living in the most peaceful time in our species' existence."[31] He cited an overall decline through past centuries of reported violent crimes and death rates from war and homicide. He talked of a decline in violent crime in the United States, specifically.

That statistic doesn't stay static. In fact, after his speech, violent crime in the USA again began to rise.[32] However, the singular factor of a violent crime rate doesn't, on its own, determine if a society is peaceful.

Consider the news headlines for a minute. We are pulling out of the recent Great Recession here in the States, but we still feel the ache of it, financially and emotionally. We are divided around the world by class, religion, politics, and color. We read about thousands of children dying each day due to malnutrition and preventable disease. Water is incredibly scarce in some areas. Strange weather anomalies come regularly and wreak havoc. Reports show considerable bribery and other corruption worldwide[33] and warn that even small increases in corruption levels can actually lead to unrest and "large declines in peace."[34]

We see animal cruelty and damage to the environment. People worry about melting ice caps and wonder how much more our earth can take. And if there's any question about how all these

---

31 Pinker, Steven. "The Surprising Decline in Violence." Speech, TED2007, 19:15. March 2007. https://www.ted.com/talks/steven_pinker_on_the_myth_of_violence?language=en.

32 Skinner, Curtis. "U.S. Crime Rate Rising, but Fewer Americans Believe It: Gallup Poll." Reuters. October 31, 2013. http://www.reuters.com/article/us-usa-poll-crime-idUSBRE99U11Z20131031.

33 "Worldwide Corruption 'on the Rise'" The Telegraph. December 9, 2010. http://www.telegraph.co.uk/news/worldnews/asia/afghanistan/8191824/Worldwide-corruption-on-the-rise.html.

34 Dawson, Stella. "Corruption Is Leading Indicator for Political Unrest, Study Finds." Reuters. May 28, 2015. http://www.reuters.com/article/us-corruption-peace-index-idUSKBN0OD23X20150528.

stressors affect us, an estimated 40 million American adults struggle with anxiety disorders.[35]

"The most peaceful time in our species' existence?" I don't think so. Just reading that list is stressful!

One thing became clear to me as I thought about the hidden dangers in Burkina Faso, Bolivia, and the United States. As I held my simple papier-mâché creation in hand, I told the children at the conference that we have to start by taking off the mask. If we want to see true peace, we have to stop "healing the wound lightly," as the book of Jeremiah says. We have to stop saying there is peace when there isn't. If we don't face problems honestly, how can we ever bring about real change?

When I first heard of Burkina Faso, I didn't know that a friend of mine would soon go to live there. I didn't know that our family would become pen pals with a five-year-old Burkinabé boy, "Little D," who sends us French-English letters with drawings of animals and fruit. That country, which I didn't even know existed, has become very important to me.

Sometimes, when I think about Little D and the challenging life he lives in his beautiful land in Africa, I think of Fernanda and Eva too. They all have odds stacked against them. We could just turn a blind eye and say, "Peace and safety to them! I'm sure they'll be all right. Children are resilient!" But they need our prayers — and, sometimes, our logistical support through programs of sponsorship, mentoring, adoption, or rescue — because things aren't always safe. Things aren't always peaceful.

These are hard stories to read. They are hard stories to live too. But we have to get used to taking off the masks. We have to address the problems. We have to be brave.

Amy Carmichael, a missionary for fifty-five years to India, was once criticized by publishers for telling negative stories along with the good ones. Too discouraging, they thought — not uplifting enough. I faced similar concerns in my heart as we wrote this book. Do I tell all of it? The hard and ugly parts? Who wants to read that?

---

[35]"Data on Behavioral Health in the United States." American Psychological Association. Accessed May 15, 2016. http://www.apa.org/helpcenter/data-behavioral-health.aspx

Yet how will sad situations improve if we don't open our eyes to see what our brothers and sisters live through every day?[36]

We are called to be peacemakers and to "strive for peace with everyone" as we also strive for holiness (Heb. 12:14 ESV). This peace, though, isn't false peace like the prophets proclaimed in Jeremiah's day, or the store employees held out as they ignored the fire, or what the government official claimed while he sent Fernanda and Eva penniless back to their house. Instead, this is true peace that comes from Christ and effects positive change.

I am much more at peace now when I am doing the hard and honest work of making things right. Every battle I fight, every time it is my turn to call out evil and stand up for good, I get a little braver. And every time God helps me to speak the truth, it adds another rock to my pile, the one that shows His faithfulness to make me strong.

What has changed in me? I now believe the truth of what God says about me, and what He says about Himself, and I live in His spirit and will instead of my own. I believe it is worth some amount of struggle and sacrifice on my part to make a difference in the world.

The name of Little D's country, Burkina Faso, means "land of upright and honest people." I wonder if he will grow to be an upright and honest man. I wonder if he will be a great leader of his family, community, or nation.

I wonder about Fernanda and Eva. I wonder about other children I have worked with, and about my own sons. May they all, as members of this next generation, choose not to wear masks that hide truth behind a lie. Instead, may they be brave and bold. May they speak the truth, and do so in love. May they — and may we — be people who bring with them real change and true peace.

---

36 Amy Carmichael finally did change something about her book—the title. She renamed it *Things As They Are* (c.f. http://www.historymakers.info/inspirational-christians/amy-carmichael.html.).

Philip, Tom, and Peter paused for a splashy picture at the La Paz Waterfall Gardens in Costa Rica.

TO BE STILL

By Janine

Silence
is hard to find
near a million strangers
in the throbbing of the city —
hot noise.

But God
is there, asking
me to find some moments
that calm me like a balmy breeze:
"Be still."

They come
on vacation —
long walks, fireplace s'mores.
No one staring, watching, looking.
Sweet rest.

Quiet
Mountain top views,
a new lamb born at dawn,
a thousand dragonfly wings at
sunset.

At times,
in the city,
serenity floats in —
Starlit porch-chair conversations —
God speaks.

Green grass,
parrots flying,
open Bible, ink pen,
wispy, hushed zephyrs are stirring…
Listen.

Breathe peace
in the bustle,
in the purpose and plan.
In a sixty-hour workweek,
Tranquil.

CHAPTER TWELVE

INTEGRITY: Constructing Character

By Tom

WHEN PETER WAS FOUR YEARS old, we enrolled him in kindergarten. Though he was on the young side, we wanted him to develop some of his social skills and interact more with other children. He was ready.

On the first day, he dressed up, and we packed his snacks. We drove him there together as a family and walked him inside, where he had his picture taken. We were excited and a bit nervous, as parents typically are.

At the end of the day, he was a bit disappointed. While he was still learning how to do things like follow the class rules and stick to a daily schedule, he felt pretty underwhelmed by it all. We had taught him to read and write small words at age three. He had a knack for it and loved to learn. So when he went to school the first day and realized they were learning alphabet letters one at a time, he didn't want to go back.

With a confident straightening of his shoulders and tuck of his lower lip, he proclaimed, "There's nothing they can teach me at that school."

When I went to kindergarten, I knew I had things to learn. But by the end of college, I felt prepared, ready, and excited for what God had in store for us.

When I got to Bolivia and began working as a missionary there,

I realized there were many things I hadn't learned. Surprisingly, many of those things didn't have to do with academics and airplane engines. They had to do with the continual construction of my character.

You see, God doesn't just leave us where we are. He has a lot of lessons left to teach me. I am so thankful for His promise that He will complete the work He began in us![37]

Kindergarteners are often asked, "What do you want to be when you grow up?"

It's a fair question. But why don't we ever ask them *who* they want to be when they grow up? What kind of men and women do they want to become? Lawyers or used-car salesmen may automatically have bad reputations due to their line of work. But a lawyer or used-car salesman with good character is much more honoring to God than a missionary or pastor with bad character.

As I have thought about good character over the years, a few directives in particular have stood out. In fact, certain lessons have come up again and again, in Bolivia and back here in the States.

Plan Ahead

While I was a missionary, a typical lunch (if there was such a thing) meant piling into a truck with the guys from the hangar and heading to one of the nearby neighborhood eateries. There, we would order plates of fried chicken with french fries, fried rice, and a two-liter bottle of Coca-Cola. It wasn't the healthiest meal, but it was cheap and it sure was tasty.

I remember one particular lunchtime when we found a restaurant with a few empty seats outdoors. From our places there, we watched some construction workers as they installed a culvert in the middle of the closed street. A young man in a yellow backhoe was digging trenches and a few others helped him from the ground.

As we ate, we were interrupted by a loud boom. A hydraulic line on the backhoe burst, sending hot hydraulic fluid all over the

---

37 Philippians 1:6

operator. He screamed in pain and then slumped over in his seat. Even though the street was closed to vehicles, there were people walking by who stopped, frozen by the noise and what had just happened.

Without a word, one of the young Bolivian mechanics at our table jumped to his feet, rushed straight into the restaurant kitchen and picked up an empty two-liter bottle. He filled it with water and ran back outside and up onto the tractor. He began to flush the hot hydraulic fluid from the man's eyes and face.

He then yelled for someone to get a taxi. He carried the man down off the tractor and loaded him into the cab, which he sent to the nearest clinic with one of the man's co-workers riding along.

I realized something as I watched Efrain's quick actions. Heroes aren't born overnight. He didn't have time to sit and consider whether or not he was going to be compassionate. He regularly made choices to think of others, and it became second nature. When the opportunity arose to act, he acted without hesitation. He was prepared.

I was in high school in the late 1980s, when First Lady Nancy Reagan was promoting the "Just Say No" campaign. The point of it was not to deliver addicts out of their drug addictions. It was designed to teach children and teens to plan ahead for the first moments when they would be tempted to do drugs. If they were ready to answer before the question was asked, Mrs. Reagan believed they had a better chance of saying no.

In the same way she hoped to help children prepare to act wisely, I've learned that I also tend to make better decisions when I know the answer before the question is asked, when I have planned ahead.

This kind of emergency preparedness is quite common in the aviation industry. If you have ever flown on a commercial airplane, then you have probably heard the flight crew tell you how to put on your seat belt and use your seat cushion for a flotation device. The flight crew does not want a crisis to happen, but they want you to have a plan, an answer before the question is asked. In a high-pressure moment, I want to be living in a way that makes me ready to jump in and do what's required.

Practice Saying No

I think that the word no might be the most difficult word to say in all of the English language. It can be hard enough to say no to things that are negative or destructive. For me, however, it is sometimes harder to say no when I'm faced with opportunities to help other people.

In a country struggling with poverty, we found needs everywhere we looked. Hundreds of children live in orphanages around the city and hundreds more, if not thousands, live on the streets. We tried to help as many people as possible, but our family sometimes got overwhelmed with the needs. Living as we should, though, is not merely about choosing something good to do. It often is about being wise and choosing what is *best* to do.

We faced that predicament frequently on the mission field. Do we take our kids on the family vacation we have planned and packed for, or do we cancel it and go to the hospital to sit with someone who is ill? Do we attend the wedding of one friend — or the funeral of another? Do we take a day to rest after a hectic workweek — or go help an overextended coworker?

Sometimes it's difficult to decide. It's tough to say no to a choice that other people would consider a good one and instead say yes to the best.

Again, it was surprising how often this kind of situation came up in aviation. In a country where buses are never considered full, and you can always fit a few more people into a taxi, it was difficult to explain why we would only allow so much weight onto our planes. It was especially complicated when some of the other flight services allowed their planes to be overloaded on a regular basis. I have seen some of those pilots pack their plane until they could not get enough lift to take off, then remove part of the weight and try again.

It was in this environment that we served the Bolivian people. Imagine telling a young mother that there was not enough room on a flight for her to bring both of her children, or telling a pastor that he would have to leave some of his Bibles or food behind as he headed to work in a remote village.

But those exceptions — a little extra weight here or flying onto a grass runway after sunset there — literally could have cost lives. Learning to say no to things that seem good is an important skill to have.

I believed it was so important that I even offered a plan to help the younger guys at the hangar learn to say it. I advised them that they could blame their refusals on me. I wanted to make sure they were not overcommitting themselves, or doing things they knew were wrong. My teammates could truthfully say, when pressed to make choices that were not their best, "I'm sorry; I can't do that. My boss won't let me."

I guess it goes back to that first step, "Plan Ahead," so that in the moment of temptation, your decisions are firm and easier. As God keeps building me, I learn more and more about how and when to say no.

Perfecting Your Sense of Balance

For a couple of seasons, especially when visiting the States, my wife and I regularly watched the television reality show *The Biggest Loser*. On this show, contestants compete at losing weight. The formula they use is a balance of food and calorie intake combined with exercise and calorie burn. It is quite effective, at least in the short term, with some contestants losing hundreds of pounds.

As I worked in fulltime ministry, I realized that the same basic formula can be used to make our lives more spiritually fit. Achieving a good balance between our spiritual "food" intake and the exercise of our spiritual gifts is vitally important to a healthy life.

What do I mean by that?

Spiritual food is what we take in as spiritual nourishment. Praying, learning more about God through reading the Bible, and fellowshipping at a Bible-believing church are some of that spiritual nourishment. Like physical food, it's essential to our growth and health.

A person who takes in food and calories without exercise, however, often becomes overweight. In the spiritual realm, people who take in biblical knowledge but never do anything with it seem gluttonous to me. They should be giving out from the things they know and have received, by helping and praying for others. When they don't, they often become self-absorbed, legalistic, and prideful.

Spiritual gifts are God-given ways to help others. They are like spiritual exercise. Throughout the history of the church, these gifts have included healing people, giving, showing discernment, teaching, speaking wisdom and knowledge, and prophesying, among other gifts (See Rom. 12 and 1 Cor. 12).

We should use the gifts God gives us according to the biblical instructions for each of them. If we are supposed to teach, we shouldn't keep that to ourselves — we should teach. If we are meant to show mercy, we should show mercy. It makes sense, doesn't it?

Yet just as taking in nourishment without exercise causes problems, exercise without proper nourishment also is extremely damaging. If we are exercising beyond our limits while eating an unhealthy diet, we become exhausted and ineffective. Spiritually exhausted people serve, give, and care, yet never seem to have time for their own spiritual nutrition. These people have plenty of time to feed the hungry, preach, teach, or help others, but they don't seem to have the time to go to church, read their Bibles, rest, or pray. We often saw this on the mission field — and I was sometimes guilty of it myself. There are so many needs that it is tempting to get out of balance. In this case, giving out without fueling back up can easily lead to burnout.

Spiritually healthy people who are mature in character learn to balance spiritual nutrition and the exercise of their spiritual gifts. I often contemplated this. Am I acting gluttonous, lazy, or selfish? Am I spiritually anorexic and exhausted? Or am I living in balance?

Many of us wish for a miracle pill or drug to lose weight and stay fit. Yet fitness — physical or spiritual — is something we have to work at continually. It is a life-long pursuit. Even those people who have been Christians for many years still need to be spiritually fed, as well as exercise their spiritual muscles serving others.

Pass Up the Pride

Shortly after we arrived in Central America for language studies, we took a test to see what class levels were appropriate for each of us. Janine had taken Spanish classes in junior high and high school, and she had been to Mexico several times. She was placed in an intermediate class. I had never studied Spanish in my life and, despite two short trips to work in a Mexican orphanage, couldn't speak more than about a dozen words. I was placed in a beginner class.

That was somewhat humbling, but it didn't matter. I was there to learn. If I had been placed in that intermediate class with Janine, I wouldn't have understood it. I couldn't have advanced the way I needed to. I had to humble myself and learn in the classes that were right for me.

Admitting I didn't know everything and couldn't do it all myself required humility. Many people who learn a second language find this out rather quickly. In the first few years, I often found myself talking with people who spoke just a bit too fast for me to follow them. If I nodded, they thought I understood, even when I didn't have a clue what they were talking about.

One day, I was talking with a security guard when he began to lose me in my limited Spanish. Yet I simply kept nodding. When we finished talking he said, "Okay, I'll see you tomorrow for dinner." My pride had kept me from admitting that I did not understand him; and I had unintentionally invited him to dinner.

Life without humility can be painful. People who can't humble themselves are often humbled despite themselves, and that is harder. The fall from a prideful position stings. I had to learn to laugh at myself, embrace my membership in the human race, admit my weaknesses, and grow. Humility enables us to go farther, faster, than pride ever will.

Persevere

My aviation training prepared me well to pull an airplane motor apart and reassemble it. It prepared me to remove a flight surface and rivet a new skin on the frame. It prepared me to rebuild a brake caliper. By the time I graduated from college, I felt quite prepared to tackle almost any repair or maintenance on a Cessna 206.

I was not so ready, however, to face the emotions I felt while helping to move the body of our national pilot's father-in-law from the plane to the back of a hearse. I wasn't quite so ready to see a young mom arrive from her small village with pregnancy complications, only to return to our hangar just a few days later with a shoe box-sized coffin. It broke my heart.

Some people who work in difficult fields — policeman, doctors, soldiers, emergency personnel, pastors, missionaries — harden their hearts against the constant losses. That is understandable. Yet I believe that God teaches us not to close ourselves off.

I didn't like to hear women wail for their loved ones. It hurt to hear the stories of orphans or watch over my wife when she was sick. It wasn't fun to sit at funerals and watch the teenagers I taught in Sunday School mourn their mothers, grandfathers, or friends. But just as there is no love without loss, there is no loss without love. The pain I felt meant that I loved them. We have meaningful relationships with people today because years ago we opened up our hearts and invested love in them.

It can be hard to persevere in love. When we put all our trust in God, however, He gives us the strength we need to stand up in empathy for our fellow human beings, over and over again. I believe He teaches and helps us to bear each other's burdens.

We got to see God do exciting things in Bolivia. Outright miracles. But I am often more amazed by things He does in my own heart. He is faithful to keep changing and loving me. As I persevere, He keeps pouring out blessings, and one of those is that He doesn't give up on me, but keeps refining me.

The famous preacher D. L. Moody once said, "Character is what you are in the dark." I think about that sometimes. Who am I when no one else but God sees me?

Do I follow through on these things I have written about? Do I prepare to stand ready against temptation? Do I say "no" when I need to? Do I have a good balance in my life, taking care of my own spiritual needs while pouring out to others in need? Do I live in humility? Do I love wholeheartedly and unselfishly, even when it hurts?

How's my character?

And how is yours? It's a good question to ask yourself. Do you steal when you know you won't get caught? Do you insult people behind their backs when you know they can't hear you? Do you speed on the freeway if there are no law enforcement officers in sight? How do you prepare and live when you are in the dark so that you will be a person of integrity in the light?

Whether you are a kindergartener or a college student, your time will be well spent if you focus on character building instead of just career building. If you want to be a missionary, don't wait until you arrive on the foreign field to do the right thing. Things will not get easier over there. Don't lie to yourself and believe that they will. If you are not walking the walk now, then you probably won't do it when you need to there. Prepare now — not just for the job you want to have, but for the person you want to be.

*Philip, Tom, and Peter enjoy a break at a waterfall
in Las Cuevas, near Samaipata, Bolivia.*

IMITATION

By Janine

OR A SEASON, I WAS *the philanthropist for a women's charity*
organization. These generous ladies worked very hard to raise
money which they would then hand over to Tom and me. We
would use it to buy groceries and other supplies for several orphanages,
delivering the goods about once a month. We felt like Santa Claus, filling
our shopping carts to capacity and then arriving at the homes with our
packages. The kids would run to greet us, filling the air with thank yous.

After working in both the charity and the orphanages for a while, I
was asked to speak at a fundraiser. I was to give a brief account of how
donor money made a difference in the lives of these children. Some of
the most powerful and wealthy people of the city were in attendance at
the benefit dinner. The women from our group were gorgeous in salon
hairstyles, silken evening gowns, and glittering accessories. Dapper
wait staff laid the tables at the four-star hotel with decadent, delicious
food. Men in suits and ties pulled out their wallets to purchase donated
paintings and airplane tickets, giving thousands of dollars to help
provide for the orphans in our care.

I was eating and chatting at my table, relaxed after my presentation
was done, when a hired band began to play. I hadn't been watching the
stage; however, after the vocals began, I just had to look up.

A group of men were doing cover versions of hits from the 1980s.
That would have been entertaining even if the band had been bad. But
they weren't bad. In fact, they were great.

What astonished me most about them was this: Whether they were
singing Rod Stewart songs or REO Speedwagon ones, they were spot on.

They performed such precise renditions, that, with closed eyes, I couldn't tell the original artists weren't singing. I wondered for a while if they were lip-syncing to recordings, but they weren't. They were the real deal. So many little tells of inflection, breathing, phrasing and accents were replicated perfectly.

What made it more amazing was that these musicians weren't North American. English wasn't their first language; Spanish was. Yet while they were singing, their English was impeccable.

I saw this knack for mimicry repeated many times in Bolivia. For example, Bolivian children learn cursive writing in much the same way that children in the States do. They receive instruction and work with patterns. However, North American children quickly put their own stamp on their worksheets. Letters vary in size, roundness, color, and the slant from left to right. There is a lot of personality, but not always an exactness to their writing. Bolivian children I worked with, on the other hand, created script that looked so uniform, so identical from page to page, that I frequently couldn't tell one person's work from another. They put in a great deal of effort to make it look just like the examples their schoolteachers showed them.

I also saw this when my family traveled out into the countryside of the Chiquitanía one day. It is an area world-renown for beautifully performed Baroque music, which was originally introduced to the Bolivian natives by Jesuit missionaries from Europe. The music has continued to be passed down for centuries.

We had lunch with some young men there, friends of friends, who had been taking violin lessons. They pulled instruments from carrying cases and began to play for us, and the living room we sat in was transformed into a great concert hall. At the end of those first few captivating minutes, we cheered and applauded the remarkable performance. Then, they played another song. And another. Stirring classical works by Bach, Tchaikovsky and others. They continued to play for an hour – without sheet music. They repeated it all, exceptionally well, from their memories of how they had heard someone else play it.

All this brought to mind a verse from the Bible that I learned years ago. "Therefore be imitators of God." (Eph. 5:1, NASB)

That Greek word for "imitators" is used a half-dozen times in the

New Testament. Each time, it refers to someone acting like another person or group of people who are inspiring and worthy of consideration. People that included Jesus. The flawless way He lived His life on this earth was worthy of respect and imitation.

How can we possibly imitate a perfect man?

The word "therefore" at the start of that verse refers back to Ephesians 4, where we read a description of ways in which we should live. The New Living Translation of Ephesians 4:25-30 says:

So stop telling lies. Let us tell our neighbors the truth, for we are all parts of the same body. And "don't sin by letting anger control you." Don't let the sun go down while you are still angry, for anger gives a foothold to the devil.

If you are a thief, quit stealing. Instead, use your hands for good hard work, and then give generously to others in need. Don't use foul or abusive language. Let everything you say be good and helpful, so that your words will be an encouragement to those who hear them.

And do not bring sorrow to God's Holy Spirit by the way you live. Remember, he has identified you as his own, guaranteeing that you will be saved on the day of redemption.

The passage ends with these instructions: "Be kind to one another, tender-hearted, forgiving each other, just as God in Christ also has forgiven you." (Eph. 4:32, NASB)

Honesty. Self-Control. Hard work. Kindness. Forgiveness. The world could use more of those things, couldn't it?

The Apostle Paul went so far as to say, "Be imitators of me, just as I also am of Christ" (I Cor. 11:1 NASB). That's pretty bold.

It reminds me of another day in Bolivia, and a particular trip to an

Ayoreo village. A Bolivian friend had taught me a song to sing with the kids, and once there, we began to lead it for them. However, the version I had heard before we left for the village was very different than the one I heard after we had arrived and stepped to the front of the room.

Since I hadn't known the song beforehand, I thought the first time through was an accurate representation of it. But the second time through, I realized we had a bit of a problem. As notes jumped, sank and squealed, I realized sadly that my friend was probably tone deaf. We were way off-key, and I didn't know how the song was actually supposed to go.

I was both amazed and horrified to hear most of the children sing along, perfectly copying the lead singer's mistakes. When the lead was flat, they were flat. When the lead was sharp, they were sharp. It was so embarrassing.

I don't think that I am where the Apostle Paul was, confident enough in my imitation of Jesus to ask a bunch of people to follow me. I don't want them to hit the sharps and flats I do as I try to live out my faith. Yet wouldn't it be wonderful one day if someone else could look at me and see a nearly-pure reflection of my Jesus, the exact representation of the glory of His Father? Wouldn't it be fantastic if my life song echoed His so closely that others could follow my footsteps to get to Him?

In the meantime, I won't be looking in the mirror for my example, but into the eyes of the One who is worthy of the work it takes to imitate Him.

CHAPTER THIRTEEN

FRIENDSHIP: LIVING IN COMMUNITY

By Janine

I LOVED MY FRIEND. I LOVED talking to her. I loved the cozy little library where we were chatting. But at that moment, I just wanted her to hush up so I could go home. I was so cold, and I had this strange sensation, as if my life were literally draining right out of me. If I didn't leave soon, I felt like I wouldn't be able to walk out of there on my own.

As soon as I was alone, I called Tom, who was just a few doors away. I couldn't wait another half-hour for him to finish his business meeting. Something was very wrong with me, and he needed to drive me home *now*. He surprised me when he said there was something wrong with him too.

In about ten minutes, we were in the truck. Tom drove, and by the time we reached our house twenty minutes away, I was shaking dramatically. He helped me to our bedroom, where I collapsed onto our bed. Then he called one of our mission doctors and began to describe our symptoms.

"Go to the hospital," the doctor directed. "I think you have dengue fever."

A mosquito-borne illness, dengue fever is common in the lowlands of Bolivia. It is often transmitted in March, April, and May, which are autumn months there. We kept our yard neat and dry, but our neighborhood was home to a murky, plant-filled drainage canal. Our neighbors had a non-working swimming pool filled with stagnant water. Insects loved both of those spots. Despite our frequent applications of repellant, we had been bitten.

We pulled ourselves together as best as we could, and Tom drove back across town. He went directly to a private hospital, where the medical attention would be good and the wait would be short. Doctors and nurses immediately went to work on me, checking my vitals, asking questions, and taking blood.

Finally, a doctor spoke to me calmly. "I don't have the results back yet," he said, "so I can't be sure. But you have symptoms of classic dengue fever. There is nothing we can do for it, nothing you can take except *paracetamol*.[38] Drink lots of water. It will last about a week. Just hold on."

In cases of dengue hemorrhagic fever, the risk of death sometimes requires more aggressive treatment, like intravenous fluids. In classic dengue, though, puncturing the skin or giving prescription medications — even ibuprofen, for that matter — can cause more damage than good. I was to rely on water, a drug like Tylenol, rest, prayer, and perseverance.

After things had stabilized some in my corner, the doctor asked if he should check Tom's vitals, as well. I said an emphatic yes. After all, Tom was very sick too. Sure enough, the thermometer showed his fever was over 104 degrees Fahrenheit.

One of our bosses urged us to move into the mission base, where there was air conditioning and an on-call nurse. We hesitated but took his advice. We must have packed some things — I don't remember. I do remember being thankful, though, for his suggestion and our decision. It didn't take long for the illness to grip us.

Dengue is a strange kind of fever that affects different people differently at different times. There are at least four known strains, and contracting one of them supposedly means you can never get that particular strain again. But you still can get the others.

Sometimes, especially in someone who is already weak, the classic illness becomes hemorrhagic. Spots appear on the gums

---

38 A British term for acetaminophen.

and skin, and bleeding begins. People die of dengue fever every year.

As the sickness runs its course, it's common for a person to have moments of strength and be able to get up and move around. There also are stages of severe exhaustion and pain where the patient can do little but lie still and groan.

We tried to sleep and rest, reading through stacks of old *Reader's Digest* magazines near our beds. During the worst of it, however, our bodies ached so badly that we couldn't sleep. Tom and I would take turns lying in bed or sitting in a rocking chair full of pillows, depending on what was most comfortable at the time. Every few minutes, we would turn like poultry on a rotisserie as the pressure of our own weight against the cushions became too much to bear.

I grew paranoid and delirious. My sense of taste was affected, and I was sure my food and drink were contaminated somehow. I stopped eating and drinking and grew dehydrated. I began to get angry that the doctors weren't there more often — even though I didn't really need them and there was nothing they could do. I was beginning to think I might die, and I really didn't care. The pain was too intense.

I would get dengue fever again the following year, and then a third time. Those two strains hit me like a long case of the stomach flu. But the first time was different. It was brutal, with headache, fever, delirium, vomiting, chills, itching feet and palms — and oh, how our muscles ached. It was as if we had been beaten. That aching is why the sickness is also known as "breakbone fever."

Through it all, community became very important. How would we have survived without it?

The people running the mission base's guest house at the time were a pair from Iowa named Dan and Neva. My husband was a brave, obedient patient for them. I was not. Those days are largely a blur for me still, but I remember ignoring nurse Neva's orders, refusing the water offered me, being weak and emotional. Yet she cared for me through all of it, getting up in the middle of the night to check on me, bringing anything I asked for and things I didn't even anticipate. She was truly a godsend to us.

So was her husband, Dan. Tom and I were given an adjoining room to our sons, who were ten and seven at the time. For a week, although they stayed right next door, we hardly saw our little boys. They would slip into our rooms to say good night or good morning, and I would try to put on a happy face and pull myself together to tell them I loved them. Dan and Neva made their lunches, washed their clothes, and fed them dinner. Dan drove them to school each day—a forty-minute round trip—and then he made sure that they got back to the base in the afternoons. I couldn't cook for my sons, or even tuck them in most nights. These precious people from our community had to help us do that.

There were others who cared for us as well. Laura brought me ice cream bonbons, when it was the only food that sounded good to me. Our mission doctors kept tabs on us—even when we didn't realize it. I have a fuzzy memory of one of our Bolivian pastors sitting beside my bed. Looking deeply concerned, he prayed in Spanish for God's healing and comfort to come to us. I believe that God heard his precious prayer.

Then there was our friend Rosa. At the end of the week, Tom was still sick, but he was gaining strength. He had followed orders. I had not, and was still feeling awful. Tom urged me to eat, but I didn't want to. Everything tasted funny, and I was still paranoid. Dehydration and hunger were becoming big problems.

Dear Rosa said she knew what I needed. She cooked a pot of delicious chicken soup from scratch and spoon-fed me. I knew it couldn't be tainted; she had made it herself. I wouldn't refuse it; I didn't want to hurt her feelings. And she wouldn't have taken no for an answer anyway.

I was on the road to recovery.

Tom and I each lost about fifteen pounds during those ten days of illness. There would be other effects as we healed, but we were loved back to better health by members of our wonderful community of friends.

Before we moved to South America, we had gone through a lot of testing, including evaluations with a counselor. His job was to determine if we were mentally fit to live as missionaries in another country. I remember one of his questions in particular: "How many friends do you need around you?"

It was an interesting inquiry. I was moving to Bolivia sight unseen. I didn't know one woman there. The counselor knew that with my existing friends thousands of miles away, and those relationships changing drastically due to the challenges of distance, I was going to need some new ones.

That wasn't easy. In fact, being away from the people I had counted on was downright painful at times. But in our years away, God provided the exact people I needed. He gave us friends who became like aunts and uncles to my children. They didn't replace our blood relatives; they added to them. God knew we would need each one.

He sent me Laurie, who made me icy caramel coffee drinks and baked goods, and always had time in her busy schedule to talk. He sent Holly, who took me treasure hunting for American treats when grocery shopping became a bit overwhelming. He sent Laura, who scouted a house for our family before we arrived and scrubbed the floors with nitric acid before we moved in. She was a set of strong shoulders I could cry on in hard moments.

Heather walked laps at the park with me, washed my dishes sometimes, and brought jokes and gifts to my sons. In our family emergencies, Joy and Bev were willing to come whenever we needed them, no matter what was happening in their own lives. Dana's kindness and wise spirit helped me refocus in moments when I got a little lost. My dear friend Jenny was the calm and reasonable "Hobbes" to the sometimes-manic "Calvin" side of my personality.[39]

Grace invited us to dinner every Thursday night until we got our feet beneath us. Virginia was a role model of attitude, continuously showing up with a smile and song on her lips. Diane and Vicki showed me around and told their own stories of culture shock and adaptation, making me feel like what I was experiencing

---

39 Reference to the characters in the famous comic strip by Bill Watterson known as "Calvin and Hobbes."

was completely normal. Beth shared my passion to minister to children, inspiring me to become a better teacher.

Those thirteen missionary ladies were there from the beginning, but many other women followed them and shared the journey with me. They were like the extended arms of my own mom, sister, aunts, and grandma when I didn't have those people near.

These women also understood this chapter of my life in a way that my friends in the States simply could not. They counseled, laughed, brought food, and prayed for me with great empathy. I remember how Laurie and Heather regularly gave me index cards on which they had written relevant Bible verses to encourage my weary heart. Those verses, tucked into mirror frames and pinned up near my computer screen, were invaluable gifts.

God sent many people with whom we built memories. With my new friends — some North American and some South American — I shared long talks, worked on construction projects, attended family events, took choral lessons, traveled, shopped in outdoor markets, ate new foods, learned new art skills, and went to spinning classes at the gym. We became part of each other's lives. I went from wondering if I would ever have friends there at all to watching God bless me time and again with soul sisters.

Was it always easy? Of course not. We didn't always get it right. As scores of North American workers came and went, and hundreds of nationals joined in ministry with and among us, mistakes were made. There were harsh words, misunderstandings, cold shoulders, broken hearts, and even some lies spoken. Like anyone else, Christians don't always do and say the right things. We are all flawed and painfully human. I was frequently reminded that a community of Christians may be full of redeemed, forgiven people, but they're not perfect.

We had to learn that love — real love — means letting go of fear. There isn't room for it. There has to be trust. Being a friend means being courageous and vulnerable. This doesn't mean we stay in toxic relationships. Yet in a world of broken people who hurt each other without trying to, there must be space for grace, forgiveness and resiliency among our true friends.

To build community, we also have to give up something else, too. We have to surrender our self-centeredness. The way our mission family poured into us when we were sick didn't come easily to them. It cost them time, energy, money, and sleep! It was a testament to their character that they laid down their own wants to put us first in that way.

Love is generous. It gives.

In turn, we got to love our friends back. We cooked meals, babysat children, planned celebrations, visited hospital rooms, loaned out our possessions and helped people move—this is just what friends do.

Circumstances in the world today have changed our attitudes about relationships, haven't they? We can be surrounded by superficial ties—with hundreds of "friends" on Facebook—and yet not have anyone to go out to eat with on a Saturday night. It is so easy these days to feel alone and empty.

To live fully means stepping out and reaching out. It means saying the hellos, shaking the hands, listening to the needs, and sharing your own stories.

Sometimes, it's really hard to know who to invest in and how. As a culture, I think we are ridiculously out of practice. Yet it is worth the effort to learn what qualities and characteristics to look for in a good friend, and then to communicate and care for a friendship once you have one.

Yes, it's hard. But what worthwhile thing isn't?

Tom and I both had the privilege of being born in the Pacific Northwest, among the mighty redwoods. As a little girl, I would hike among them, build forts with my sister, and lie on my back watching sunlight filter down among the enormous swaying arms of those giant trees. I remember how the leaves they dropped to earth were not like the wide leaves of deciduous trees in autumn. They weren't crackly, colorful and crisp. Instead, their little flat spikes formed a thick, soft, brown carpet that absorbed my footsteps and quieted the forest floor.

The seasons would pass, and the fallen needles would eventually be replaced on the branches with young growth. I would press the feathery, new, light green tips hard against my fingers to make an impression of ridges on my skin.

Sequoia sempervirens can thrive for millennia and are documented as the tallest living things in the entire world. These trees can reach 350 feet or more in height, about the size of a thirty-story hotel. They are big enough that the four members of our family have stood inside some hollowed out by lightning or men to make living buildings and car tunnels.

Amazingly, though, these enormous trees have relatively small and shallow roots.

Their stability comes in standing together. The roots of one entwine, and sometimes even fuse, with the roots of other redwoods nearby. Together, they withstand floods, earthquakes, and windstorms. Together, they take in moisture and nutrients that they need to survive.

Isn't that a powerful metaphor for us, too? Alone, we could have easily toppled as we moved back and forth between countries, thrown down sometimes by the winds and rain that are a part of life. But God sent friends whose roots entwined with ours and even fused in places. We stood strong, side by side.

As we look at the incredible world around us, we see this connection of community. From groves of redwood trees to hives of bees, waddles of penguins to wolf packs, nature is designed this way. It's part of the plan. And it's worth the risks.

It certainly was for us.

*During a jungle trip, while waiting for part of our
team to arrive, Peter entertained village children by
driving some of his toy cars around in the dirt.*

*In a different village, Philip (in the center of the boat) took
a ride on an Amazonian tributary with local children.*

SERENATAS

By Janine

ONE OF THE FIRST NIGHTS *of our year-long stay in Costa Rica, we were jolted awake to the sound of "Happy Birthday," forcefully played mariachi-style on a very loud trumpet. This was followed, on a different night, by a boisterous moonlit love song and wedding proposal from a man we didn't know to our female neighbor.*

Coming from a country with noise ordinances and laws about disturbing the peace, all this pre-dawn ruckus was rather unsettling to us. Even annoying. Why couldn't the neighbors be more respectful of people sleeping?

I mentioned my frustration to one of our Costa Rican friends, and she was baffled by my reaction. "What's not to love?" She asked me. She was positively sentimental at the thought of her countrymen marking important celebrations by singing to each other outside, on dark, starry nights.

We didn't see it that way. We didn't get it.

Why couldn't they sing in the daytime? Didn't that make more sense? There is a reason the sun goes down at night – so we can sleep!

Then we moved to Bolivia, and soon, the house that was surrounded by music was ours.

At first, honestly, we still didn't really understand or appreciate it. We learned the routine but failed to comprehend the reasons. Why roust someone from bed to wish them well?

Our patient friends walked us through the serenade pattern that first year or two. First came the phone call, to someone in the house who wasn't the honoree. Would we be home? Would the birthday boy or girl

171

be asleep? Apparently, it ruins the fun if the guest of honor stays up until midnight, waiting for the serenade.

I probably should pause here for a confession. I played along, but was sometimes one of those people who ruined the fun. Knowing a carful of guests – some of them possibly strangers – would soon come to sing to me led me to some changes in my nightly routine. I exchanged my pajamas for sweatpants and a t-shirt. I kept my makeup on and tried not to muss my hair too much, while resting on top of the bedcovers instead of beneath. I slept lightly, listening for their arrival on our street. I was definitely one of those honorees who tried to stay awake.

The first song was always sung at the property perimeter. We would come to the gate and open it, but our friends would remain outside – even in cold or rain – in keeping with their tradition. Then, when they were ready (usually around the third song), they would come indoors and sing some more. If we really did sleep through several songs and they were stuck outside waiting for too long, they would call on a cell phone to wake us up.

Inside, the fun continued. They kept singing, including any song chosen by the guest of honor, no matter how sweet or silly. Then there were words of blessing, jokes, and finally a prayer. Snacks were served, and sometimes a cake was offered. The whole thing generally took about an hour – from midnight to 1 a.m.

It didn't take too many of these evenings to melt my heart. These people had parents, siblings, and children to care for; jobs to go to; classes at university to attend the next day. They were really busy, most of them. But they voluntarily gave up hours of their own sleep to come and sing to us. They sometimes had to pay cab fare. They often squished at least seven people into a tiny car. They drove through rough neighborhoods and down muddy streets full of potholes. They never skipped a year.

Once there was a garbage strike, and the wind blew the smell to our front door. Our friends sang anyway, faces covered. That was the only year they rushed inside after the first song.

Another time, there was a tremendous storm. Although showers didn't usually stop them, this particular tempest was intense, with flooding. So instead of coming in person, they called in the middle of the night and sang to me for about ten minutes while clustered around a cell phone.

They came on Tom's birthday. They came on mine. They came on Mother's Day, too. On that night, they went from house to house among friends, singing to about twenty moms, handing out flowers with their music. They were up half the night giving this gift to others. Some nights, they would be falling asleep as they chatted. But they came.

We usually weren't expected to go serenading because our house was far from the others and our children had to be up early in the morning for school. But participating in some of those adventures became some of my most cherished memories.

Our first night as serenaders, we ate cheese sandwiches on flattened white bread, with store-bought cookies and crackers. We drank extra-sweet coffee from plastic cups so thin that mine was literally melting and warping in my hand. Tom and our friend, Elvio, each gave the sleepy guest of honor a meaningful birthday blessing. Then, after singing and visiting, we hugged him and left.

I realized that night, surrounded by friends, that I would miss some things dearly if we returned to live in the United States. Like serenatas. *Those things we once perceived as rudeness had finally become precious to me.*

I would miss the way Elvio does the little echoes and trills in the songs. The way the Rodriguez sisters' strong, confident voices fill in empty spaces. I would miss the way Andrea laughs. The way her husband Guillermo and friend Silder add bits in Portuguese and make everyone else laugh. I would miss Doly's sweet exclamations of "a-men" and the way Richard takes the guitar playing to a different level. I would miss watching our pastor play the Bolivian calfskin drum and how the group watched for our expressions whenever they tried to sing "Happy Birthday" to us in English.

It's all really quite fantastic. And the longer I lived in Latin America, the more I appreciated it.

I was wrong back in Costa Rica. Today, I finally get it. Today, I am grateful for love. For good friends. For music, prayers, and laughter.

For sweet coffee in thin plastic cups.

CHAPTER FOURTEEN

JOY: A CLEARER VISION

By Tom

F IREMEN HAVE ALARMS TO ALERT them to emergencies. Police have sirens. Our flight crew at SAMAIR Bolivia had telephones and a high-frequency radio. When the phone rang, we had no idea what to expect.

One lazy Saturday, the pastor of a small church in eastern Bolivia called, and his story was a hard one to hear. A small child had been injured while helping clean up the church yard and needed medical attention immediately.

The child lived in a quiet town that was hundreds of years old and lined with dirt roads, carved wooden pillars, boardwalks, and storefronts. Walking through, it was almost as common to see horse-drawn carts as it was to see motorcycles or taxis. Shade trees in the plaza and hammocks on the patios helped residents endure the heat. A lake enticed swimmers—at least those who weren't afraid of the piranhas that lived there.

This town was only about two hours from Santa Cruz by air, but a dozen hours by land. Time was ticking. So our pilot Greg headed east to get the patient, while I stayed behind at the hangar to maintain communication with him and the boy's family.

The plane returned several hours later and touched down on the grass airstrip. It rounded the corner to pull into the hangar, and I noticed a small boy about eight years old inside the plane.

He had a white patch over his eye and an enormous smile on his face.

As the story unfolded, I learned that the church had organized a work day to clean up some of the yard, and Pablo and his friend were using machetes to clear brush. As his friend was swinging his machete, Pablo walked up behind him and caught the point of the long knife right square in his eyeball. The small infirmary in their little town was not equipped to deal with the injury, so we were called to bring him to the "big city doctors."

I offered Pablo, his father, and older sister a ride to the hospital, and we headed off in my Land Cruiser. Pablo's uncovered eye never stopped scanning, as he excitedly pointed out the crowds, cars, and buildings of the city. He didn't complain, cry, or scream. He was perfectly calm.

We rushed him into the hospital and waited for the surgeon. The family had no money to pay for an operation, but as news of the accident and their financial need spread through the missionary community and the Bolivian church association we worked with, funds began coming in. There was no guarantee that surgery would heal him. If he could be operated on soon, however, there was a small chance that he might keep at least part of the sight in his injured eye. Pablo was very young, and people wanted to give him that chance.

The next day, Philip and I headed to the hospital to check on the patient. It was a hot day and, inside the recovery room, humidity dripped down the four bare concrete walls. Pablo and his family members all sat on one of two antiquated metal hospital beds that were the only furniture in the room. They had chosen the one under the lone open window.

In that gloomy environment, two things stood out: the new white patch that was taped over Pablo's eye, and his huge grin.

The surgery had gone well, but they would not know whether Pablo had lost his sight until they removed the bandage the following week. I visited him and his dad a few more times through that week, once bringing crayons and a coloring book to keep him entertained during the long wait. Never once in that week did

175

I ever hear the young boy complain; never did his demeanor or countenance fade.

Then the anticipated day came. With great expectation, I sat in the waiting room while Pablo and his father went into the operating room with the surgeon to have the bandages removed. After what seemed like hours, the trio emerged with a fresh patch over Pablo's eye and another huge smile on his face.

I asked him how the surgery went, and with that same great positivity, he said, "I can't see a thing!"

I wanted to cry. I felt horrible—for his loss and for what he would miss out on as he grew. But I felt even worse when I realized how I lacked Pablo's joy. I knew James 1:2, the verse that tells us to consider it joy when we face trials of many kinds. I had even memorized it in Spanish with the Sunday school class I taught.

But while Pablo was actively practicing that verse, I struggled to find joy in this circumstance. In the days that followed, I realized that, although I was not the one who lost sight in an eye, I was wrestling with the boy's situation and feeling sorry for him.

He was partially blinded, but joy oozed from every pore of his body. How could that be?

It surely didn't come from his circumstances. It was something rooted way down deep in his heart, and circumstances couldn't change it. He trusted God with *everything* in his life.

I have seen God answer many prayers, but honestly I was disappointed he did not answer this one. Actually, this wasn't even the first time I had prayed for someone's sight to be restored, and He hadn't answered the way I had hoped on that one either.

Janine's friend Veronica had asked me one day if I could help her husband Jorge get an appointment with one of the mission doctors. Jorge had been fighting the effects of diabetes for years and was slowly losing his eyesight.

The doctor was blunt.

"You must change your diet immediately," she said. "If you do not eat less sweets, carbohydrates, and starch, you will continue to lose your eyesight. You have probably already lost some feeling in your toes, and you can't feel mosquitoes biting you, either, can you?"

She knew what she was talking about.

Both Jorge and his wife seemed unfazed by the doctor's news, even stating that it would be too difficult to change his diet. Over the next few years, Jorge's health continued to decline until he was completely blind. He struggled with other effects of the illness as well.

One morning after church, Jorge asked me to sit next to him. He wanted to talk. He began to tell me of a dream that he had. In it, I had prayed for him, and his eyesight was restored. He asked me to pray for him like I had in the dream, so that God would restore his sight. I have never felt such pressure to pray and have God answer my prayer in all my life.

I sat next to Jorge and prayed and waited. But God didn't heal him. Instead, Jorge had to learn to live with his new circumstances. Jorge had to continue being a good husband, wise dad, and caring grandpa. He served the Lord and his church when he could, sharing words of encouragement and teaching, or singing songs with his deep soothing voice. He kept studying the Bible while listening to it on cassette tape — all without his eyesight.

Did I not ask in enough faith? Was I not good enough? Was God not big enough? Did God no longer do healings?

Or were those specific prayers for sight not answered because God had different plans for Pablo and Jorge?

The apostle Paul — one of the great heroes of the Christian faith — also asked God to heal him and was denied. God dramatically delivered Paul from his previous life of legalism and other wickedness done in the name of religion. He put him to work leading the growing group of people following Jesus's teachings about love and forgiveness. God even gave Paul remarkable revelations about heaven. Then He gave Paul something he didn't want — a "thorn in the flesh" that wouldn't go away, something that humbled him and caused him trouble.

Paul describes it like this: "Therefore, in order to keep me from becoming conceited, I was given a thorn in my flesh, a messenger of Satan, to torment me. Three times I pleaded with the Lord to take it away from me. But He said to me, 'My grace is sufficient for you, for My power is made perfect in weakness.' Therefore

I will boast all the more gladly about my weaknesses, so that Christ's power may rest on me. That is why, for Christ's sake, I delight in weaknesses, in insults, in hardships, in persecutions, in difficulties. For when I am weak, then I am strong" (2 Cor. 12:7b-10 NIV).

Nobody knows for sure what Paul's thorn was—the Bible doesn't tell us. Some have suggested Paul had vision problems. We know he could relate to eye problems; he was blinded on the road to Damascus, so he had lost his sight at least temporarily. He also writes to the Galatians about an illness he had while he was with them and says, "If possible, you would have plucked out your own eyes and given them to me" (Galatians 4:15b NKJV). Later, he emphasizes to them that he is writing in large letters with his own handwriting. In Acts 23, he does not recognize the high priest in the Sanhedrin, possibly because of poor eyesight.

Paul may have endured some kind of illness that caused long-term vision loss similar to the loss that the accident caused in Pablo. It's possible that, like Jorge, the apostle was praying to have his sight back. But we really can't tell for sure from these passages. We don't know.

Although we don't know what ailment Paul wanted removed, we do know something very powerful about this "thorn." Whatever it was, Paul accepted it with joy.

Where his letter says, "I was given a thorn," he uses a Greek word for "given" that means just that. Paul doesn't say this hardship was inflicted on him, shackled to him, or forced on him. It was *given* to him. It is an ancient word that refers to giving someone something that they need, or even bestowing on them a gift.

Did Paul see his thorn as a gift? What did he—the one who had this thorn that God would not take away—think of suffering and unanswered prayers? What did he have to say about responding to unwanted and unwelcome trials and circumstances in our lives?

Through the thirteen letters we know that Paul wrote for the New Testament, we get a glimpse of how he thought we should live during unsettling and unwanted challenges, in those moments when God doesn't answer us the way we think that He should.

Paul told the Romans, "Keep your spiritual fervor, serving the Lord. Be joyful in hope, patient in affliction, faithful in prayer" (Rom. 12:11b-12 NIV).

Similarly, he wrote to the Corinthians, saying that God's wisdom was different than their human thoughts, and that there was more planned for them than just their lives on this earth.

Paul was in prison when he wrote to the church in Philippi. He actually told them that his chains were for the benefit of the church. Instead of whining and complaining, he wrote about being hopeful, content in all circumstances, and confident that he could do all things through Christ, the One who gave him strength. He encouraged the Philippians toward unity and fellowship, focus on Christ, and prayer instead of worry. Over and over again, he says one word in particular: Rejoice.

He is in prison and he says to rejoice.

When we ask for something good—such as healing for our friends—and God says no, it is tempting to doubt. It is human nature to wonder if He loves us, hears us, and is powerful enough to do what He says. But God often—*often*—works in ways we don't see or understand.

We can fight Him or trust Him. Paul understood there was more going on than he could see. He trusted God and rejoiced. Little Pablo rejoiced too. He has only one functional eye now. But that circumstance didn't destroy his heart. His physical vision has changed for the worse, but maybe his spiritual vision has deepened.

Mine sure has.

Tom met a sloth who was roaming the grounds at the zoo.

GRATEFUL

By Janine

T HE SHOPPING CENTER KNOWN AS *La Feria Barrio Nueva Linda — or "the Feria" for short — resembles a noisy, odoriferous American flea market. Clothing, handmade furniture, food, and household supplies can all be found twice a week at the Feria.*

Men and women who are crippled, blind, or otherwise infirm line the outer walls. They try to get a few coins to fall into their cups, hands, hats, and boxes. Inside the building, wending their way through the crowds, independent salesmen and thieves search for money too.

People push in from every angle. But one man in the midst of the hundreds astonished us. He sat inside the Feria, almost always positioned in the same spot, in one of the widest aisles. Hundreds and thousands of people passed him as he sat there on the filthy floor.

He had lost his legs somehow. He sat in a wheelchair and played an old, beat-up guitar. Due to what appeared to be arthritis, his fingers were too twisted to hold a pick to play. So he strummed with an unbreakable plastic comb. We knew him by the joy in his heart, the smile on his face, and his music. Week after week, he sat in that dirty, crowded place and loudly sang the song we came to love: "Gracias, gracias, Señor! Gracias, mi Señor Jesus!"[40]

The song, recorded by Marcos Witt, talks about God giving a man salvation and overflowing his soul with love. The man doesn't know how to thank God for all He has done for him, and all he can give back to God at that moment is his song.

---

40 "Thank You, thank You, Lord! Thank you, my Lord Jesus!"

This is the melody and message we heard echoing through our hearts so many days, sung by a legless man in a dim hallway in the most impoverished country in South America. "Gracias. Gracias, Señor. Gracias, mi Señor Jesús!"[41]

Once, as we sang the song with our church during a Good Friday service, I looked around at the people gathered near a pool being used for baptisms. One woman had been recently widowed from her husband. Another woman was estranged from hers. A third woman, pale-faced and quiet, was bearing a terrible secret few knew — she had recently miscarried much-wanted twins. I thought about how we all bear the scars of this world that we live in, and how I am not an exception. But I also thought about how we — even if we are limbless like the man in the Feria — have so much to thank God for.

It is not only that things could be worse — which, of course, they always could be. But it is also that most of the time, if we look around and count our blessings, our lives really are good. Most of the time, we have someone to love, or good health, or a warm house, or a decent job, or a sympathetic ear, or an enjoyable hobby, or food in our bellies — or all those things put together. And even when things don't feel wonderful — even in the dark, lonely, and depressing times — we ache because our soul knows we lack a heavenly justice and loveliness. We know there is more than the darkness can see. We can hope and look forward to better days coming.

We can be grateful — and even rest and rejoice — in the middle of tough seasons, because our God is available to carry us through the hard spots. And we can be grateful knowing that we do not have a God who is weak, mean, or unsympathetic, but One who has felt loss even deeper than our own. He knows rejection, He knows profound sadness, He knows frustration and anger at injustice. He is mightier than all of it.

The term Good Friday *seems like a misnomer. The day Jesus died seems like the worst of all bad days. But we rightly call it good because it is a day for which we as Christians can and should be inexplicably thankful!*

I don't know where or how the guitar man is today, the man who was too busy singing of the goodness of God to complain. But we remember

---

41 Witt, Marcos. "Gracias." Lyrics published in 1995. Venció En Vivo, CanZion Producciones.

him often, when we hear the song he sang or think about joy in adversity. I still feel his smile of encouragement in my own heart.

May I daily remember to stop to take notice of God's gifts of goodness and grace. I have so much each day for which to be grateful.

CHAPTER FIFTEEN

GROWTH: LESSONS LEARNED
ABOUT POVERTY

By Janine

ABOUT TWO DECADES BEFORE I was born, my grandparents started a church in a mountain community. With others who worked alongside them, they spent time, energy, and money helping their neighbors for more than thirty years. Grandpa and Dad preached to the adults. Grandma, Mom, and my aunts and uncles welcomed and taught the children. My mom also played the organ and led a children's choir.

I spent my first twelve years as part of that congregation.

It was a giving church. We sent financial gifts to people working in foreign lands. My grandmother fed local children from her kitchen. We were taught to donate some of our gently used clothes and toys to others. We invested in the local rescue mission, giving not only money but also some of our time. We were committed to encouraging the homeless in our community as they struggled to get back on their feet.

I was raised to be a giver.

By the time I had arrived in Bolivia, however, something had changed in me. My thoughts on poverty and the people who were poor had changed. Looking back, I think this transformation started during my high-school years as I let myself be swayed by attitudes and beliefs I saw acted out around me.

The first was a national trend. A televangelist who preached sermons into our living rooms gave tours of his magnificent ministry complex. Its tall columns led to high ceilings and modern skylights. Amid waterslides and a stylish hotel, he made constant pleas for more money.

Another televangelist was building a grand cathedral on the opposite coast. In the winter, live camels came indoors for the Christmas play, and actors dressed as angels swayed in rigging overhead.

Luxurious lifestyles seemed to be prevalent among "blessed" preachers like these, as millions of dollars flowed like wine. I don't think that most of these men intended harm. They probably believed the prosperity theology they taught. They did good things and helped many people, despite those spending habits that now seem ridiculous. But the frequent begging for more—asking hardworking men and women to pay for fancy cars, private plane rides, and upper-class houses—affected me somehow.

By the time I entered college, that line of reasoning echoed a lot closer to home. Our family's country chapel, with its gladiolas in front and berry bushes and chicken coops out back, had been very simple. There were no stained-glass windows, no paved or labeled parking spaces, no kitchen. There wasn't even a bathroom, unless we went next door to Grandma's house. A little foyer led to the main room, which could seat about fifty on uncushioned wooden pews.

When my grandparents closed the doors on that little church after three decades, we merged with another congregation in town. I loved attending this new church, learned a lot, and made many new friends. Tom and I even met there. I fell in love with mission outreaches and grew deeper in my faith and knowledge of the Bible.

Shortly after we arrived, however, the church began a building project. The congregation had been renting multiuse spaces, and the time had come to purchase a place of our own. As a family, we helped prepare for the proposed new building.

But suddenly, some of the people in our new congregation

were fixated on things like color and pile length of the carpet. There was talk about how God wanted us to have not just essential things, but luxurious things. I remember looking up at an elaborate chandelier donated for the lobby and wondering, *This, too?* It was a far cry from the simple, wood-shake-shingled sanctuary at my grandparents' church.

The project eventually ended badly, in a church split, debt, and foreclosure. But not before I got the notion in my head—from people that I trusted—that God wanted us to have nice things, that they were a sign of His favor on us and our church.

Let me be clear: Our church did not teach prosperity theology — the belief that God will give us any material wealth for which we ask as long as we have enough faith. I don't think I would have agreed with that, if it had been presented to me directly. I don't believe our pastors believed that. My parents certainly did not. Yet the idea still came back to me in a few offhand comments by other members of the congregation that we were showing love for God by making His house elegant. After all, didn't the famous King Solomon build such a place at God's own request?

I began to dismiss the poor. If they served God, wouldn't they be blessed too? Wasn't poverty their choice? We worked hard, believed in the Bible, and were blessed. Wasn't their situation really up to them?

Someone shared a verse with me from the book of Second Thessalonians that said, "For even when we were with you, we commanded you this: If anyone will not work, neither shall he eat" (3:10 NKJV). Again, it was their choice to go without, wasn't it?

There was a story from the book of Mark: Two days before Jesus was to die on the cross, a woman poured expensive perfume on Him, which was symbolic of preparing His body for burial. The treasurer of Jesus' group, Judas, wanted more money for himself. So, because he was upset that he hadn't got his hands on the money that the woman spent, he said that she had wasted the perfume. He complained that it could have been sold and the money spent on "the poor."

Jesus answered back, "You will always have the poor among you... You will not always have me" (Mark 14:7 NLT).

Jesus didn't sound so preoccupied with the poor, did He? If you don't work, you don't eat. The righteous are blessed. The perfume was to be spent on Jesus, not the poor. Why should I be concerned about the poor if Jesus Christ didn't seem to be?

During those teenage years, I went to Mexico four times with a choir from our church. I occasionally saw deep marks of poverty as I worked and traveled there. Our trip directors intentionally showed us cardboard shacks people lived in, to open our hearts and minds to the needs of others. Yet, our job on those trips was primarily caring for emotional and spiritual needs, which we did well. When I came home, I filed those other images away and focused on the good things, the lives that were changed for the better while we were there. After a while, I only thought occasionally about the people dwelling in those cardboard shacks.

My experiences in Bolivia some fifteen years later were quite different. I couldn't forget the faces of the hungry there so easily because I lived among them.

I remember the first time I went with my husband and children to see the Plaza 24 de Septiembre. Arguably the most-visited tourist site in the city, it was graced by palm and toborochi trees, shoe shiners, drink sellers, taxis, newspaper vendors, and a gorgeous Catholic cathedral. It was a tranquil, restful place.

Yet it was there, during our first week in the country, that we were confronted with the poverty and alcoholism that we would see time and again during our stay. A man lay on the sidewalk, his pants dropped to his thighs, surrounded by his own excrement. Businesspeople stepped around him without stopping.

Down that same street, Calle Ayacucho, a row of beggars asked for food and money from passersby. One woman in particular caught our attention. She begged with two newborn infants in her arms. Over time, we saw her twin children grow from babies to lively toddlers, their own little hands finally ready and willing to take coins.

As the years passed, we were approached by people at our

home, on the street, in our car, in front of our office building, and even at restaurant tables while we dined. Once, in a crowded marketplace, I was punched in the leg. I had not seen a man's hand jutting out at me, asking for alms. His thrown fist got my attention.

Economically speaking, Bolivia has been the poorest country in South America for at least twenty years in a row. While we were there, it also was consistently the third poorest country in the whole Western Hemisphere. Since average incomes in the United States are about twenty times that of their Bolivian counterparts,[42] we often faced questions: South Americans asked what it was like to be rich (we were living just above the US poverty line), and North Americans asked how we dealt with the poor around us.

I have to admit that second question especially made me do some soul-searching. How should we deal with the problem of poverty? Even with my newly discovered prejudices, I found it abhorrent to consider ignoring it. I was there to show all of these people the love of God. But where is the line between compassion and codependency? Was it my responsibility? Do we help them if we feed the destructive cycle of slothfulness by giving them food and money they don't earn? What happens if we leave the country and our care for them stops?

Daily, women would wander the streets of wealthy and middle-class neighborhoods, pulling things from outdoor trashcans to keep, sell, or recycle. Sons and daughters would dress in native costume and beg or sell goods alongside their parents instead of going to school. At Christmastime, truckloads of people from out of town would travel to our city where the begging was better, and they could bring home more cash with less effort. Little children would rush out in the streets, recklessly weaving between busy traffic to juggle limes, knowing some drivers would hand loose change out their windows.

What was the answer?

42"List of Countries by past and Projected GDP (nominal) per Capita." Wikipedia. Accessed May 15, 2016. https://en.wikipedia.org/wiki/List_of_countries_by_past_and_projected_GDP_%28nominal%29_per_capita#IMF_estimates_between_2010_and_2019.

We had hits and misses as we tried to do the right thing. Once, Tom was approached while stopped at a red light. Inside his car, he had a group of visiting North Americans and a big bag of oranges. Outside, a young man was asking for food and holding a cup of contact cement that he was huffing.

We knew boys from this street. We worked with a care home that fed and sheltered them when they were willing to leave behind their drugs and violence. The director of that home would drive this route often, reminding the boys where they could come for help. They had hope if they would take hold of it. They just needed the faith and courage to walk away from where they were.

Sadly, some of these youths were still too captivated by the idea of their wild lifestyle. Even though they were starving, beaten, sick, freezing in the winter, and despairing nearly to madness at times, some would not give in. We would sometimes pray for them to reach the bottom quickly, so they would finally look up, ask for help, and begin to rebuild their lives.

This appeared to be one of those trapped boys.

Tom held an orange in his hand but reached out for the container of glue.

"Give me the glue," he said, "and I'll give you food."

The young man reached for the orange, but clung to his addiction.

The light would change soon, but Tom knew this was a crisis moment. He needed to try to cut through the fog and make this man think. He needed to choose, to reach a point where he saw that two roads were in front of him every day — one leading to life and one leading to death.

But he wouldn't unclench his fingers from what he was holding.

"You need to choose. You don't want that. You want this," Tom pressed. "Give me the glue, and you can eat!"

The North Americans in the car were stunned and shaken. One's eyes brimmed with tears. My husband knew that opinions were mixed, and that others didn't approve of his withholding the fruit.

The light changed. Tom tried again. The man turned away, still hungry and high.

What was the right thing to do?

I can't say with 100-percent clarity when to give money to panhandlers and when not to do so. I can't tell you who will or won't drink away the coins received, who is starving, and who just bums money for fun on their lunch break from school. A common trick we saw among one tribal group was for young girls to carry around other people's babies to garner sympathy. How can we know the truth?

We contended so much with this topic and were asked about it so often that I took a hard look at my philosophy of poverty. What did I believe and why? Had anything changed in my heart as I interacted with hungry, crippled, and needy people day after day?

I began to lay aside those foolish, childish thoughts about prosperity that were planted in my teens, the ones that had sprouted like weeds and uprooted what my family had tried to instill in me. What about living and giving sacrificially for others? What is my role in this huge problem of global poverty? Do I need to have a role at all?

I believe in the Bible. It may seem like just an old book, but it is true and brimming with inspired wisdom for today. I started there, running my modern ideas from friends, pastors, political commentators, and celebrities through the grid of God's sacred words. In the end, a lot of the Bible's teaching on poverty boiled down to six principles. And they weren't exactly the ones I had defaulted to in my youth. In fact, some of the verses that people had quoted to me had been taken far out of context.

For example, Solomon's temple had indeed been built lavishly to reflect love and honor for God. What I didn't hear, however, was the truth that after the destruction of Solomon's temple, God declared His *people* – not a building – to be the structure in which He would dwell. Who was talking about that part of the story? It is a good thing to have a church building that is clean and beautiful and representative of a God that blesses us. But extravagance? Is that really necessary when we, not an empty building, constitute God's dwelling place?

And, yes, the verse from Second Thessalonians is based on a

sound principle. People who could work, yet didn't do so, forfeited their right to eat. I found it interesting, though, that the apostle Paul directed this statement toward churchgoers who weren't working, not primarily at people outside of the church.

Remember what Jesus said in the story of the woman who anointed Him with perfume? Yes, it was indeed true that poor people were going to be around a long while, and continue to live among the disciples of Jesus. It was true that Jesus was more important and more of a priority. Yet, that was far from all God had to say on the subject. The verse from Mark was not saying that poor people were not a concern for hardworking Christians. That is a pitiful and incorrect interpretation.

The verse actually refers back to a similar one in the fifth book in the Old Testament which says, "There will always be poor people in the land. *Therefore I command you to be openhanded toward your fellow Israelites who are poor and needy in your land*" (Deut. 15:11 NIV, emphasis mine). It was a command to give, not an excuse not to do so.

When that passage is echoed in the book of Mark, Jesus was about to ascend to heaven. He told His followers, "The poor you will always have with you, *and you can help them any time you want.* But you will not always have Me" (Mark 14:7 NIV, emphasis mine).

It's not that people weren't supposed to help the poor; the point was that they needed to take care of Jesus first. God is to be of first importance over everything else — including our efforts to help the poor. It reminds me of the advice given on plane trips. In case of emergency, adult passengers are instructed to put on their own oxygen masks first, then help their children with theirs. It's not that they aren't supposed to help their children; they just need to do it in the correct order. Spiritually, we need to make sure we are right with God before we go out to try and make things right with people.

I had a lot to learn.

Remember those six principles I mentioned? The ones from the Bible that tell what God thinks about the poor? They go something like this:

1. Jesus cares about the poor, and makes it clear we should care too. (cf. Prov. 19:17)

2. God is especially interested in the care of widows and orphans, who can't as easily care for themselves. (cf. James 1:27, Ps. 68:5)

3. If we can work, but choose not to, we give up our right to eat. (cf. 2 Thess. 3:10; Prov. 12:11, 13:4)

4. The spiritual is always more important than the physical. (cf. Matt. 6:25, 10:28, I Tim. 4:8)

5. We shouldn't ignore physical needs when offering spiritual help. (cf. James 2:15-16).

6. We should give to all who ask, but our gifts might not be financial. (c.f. Luke 6:30, Acts 3)

That last principle is one that I have thought about a lot. Luke 6:30 tells us to give to all who ask, but it does *not* tell us to give them exactly what they ask for. It's common sense that what they want may not be what they need. There are times when giving food or money is exactly right. We are to be wise, however. Sometimes — with addictions or in potentially violent situations, for instance — giving food and money is entirely inappropriate.

There is an ancient story of a lame man in Israel who was begging for money one day at an entrance to the Jewish temple. The apostle Peter saw him there and told him, "I have no silver and gold, but what I do have I give to you. In the name of Jesus Christ of Nazareth, rise up and walk!" (Acts 3:6 ESV) Peter didn't have money to give, but he had the gift of healing, so he healed the man. Healing — spiritual and physical — was what the lame man really needed.

There is another interesting principle to notice in this story as well. Right before Peter heals the man, the Bible says, "Peter looked straight at him, as did John." (Acts 3:4 NIV) They saw the lame man. They looked in his face. They didn't hide or turn away.

How often, instead of seeing the person in front of us, do we just focus on the issue of money? We give cash or just drive away — often doing what is easy and gets us out of there quickly. That definitely has been my response plenty of times.

After all my soul-searching, the biggest shift in my philosophy about the poor wasn't in selecting a particular percentage of my money to give, or deciding who deserved it and who didn't. It wasn't even coming up with meaningful speeches to give those asking for help. It was about seeing them — looking into their eyes and making a decision, instead of looking away. I believe with my whole heart that God *sees* the poor; He doesn't just have a political or social opinion about them.

Sometimes I think of the Gustavo Gutierrez quote that another missionary shared with me: "You say you care about the poor? Then tell me, what are their names?"

Do I *see* them?

Sometimes I think about my brave friend Marco Antonio, working long days on an empty stomach to feed his hungry family.

"Some days, it's hard," he told me once. "But it's ridiculous to complain about it. So I drink a big glass of water, count my blessings, and get back to work."

He isn't just a statistic. He's a man, with a family, struggles, and hope.

Sometimes I think of that woman begging with her twins, sitting on a piece of concrete on Ayacucho Street. I wonder about her parents. Were they around to raise her? Did they teach her to reach for more? I wonder about her babies' father. Where is he? I wonder what brought her to the place where she is, and if she wants to change her circumstances. I wonder what her children will do with the precious gift of life they have been given.

Sometimes I think of Bill, one of the men from the rescue mission who ate in our home when I was a little girl. He had sobered up, found a job, and become our friend. I occasionally get frustrated by the transients in our town who arrogantly ask for us to pay for their coffee, cigarettes, drugs, and beer. Then I remember. While some of them revel and wallow in their lifestyle, I remember Bill's passion to do better, regain his relationships with family, have purpose, and be a respected man. I no longer see all of the homeless as the same, but as individuals.

And I think of my own little family and twenty years of financial ups and downs. We have faced multiple thefts of our possessions, seasons of unemployment, college bills, hospital expenses, a stock-market crash, dreams put on hold, and questions about the future. Life is full of twists and turns. I realize that every breath and dollar we have is a divine gift.

How do I feel about poverty now? I think we are all closer to it than we may realize. We should work diligently and gratefully.

How do I see the poor now? I hope that I see them more like Christ sees me — unique and precious. If I view them like that, I think my actions will likely follow in an appropriate way.

When I see value in them, it encourages me to judge less and to ask God for guidance more. It prompts me to surprise someone with a gift card or meal. It inspires me to carry a pair of warm socks in my car in case a stranger needs them. It moves me to donate to a rescue mission or to direct people to a reputable church that will help in a more holistic way than I can by myself. For friends in trouble, I can help print their resumes or drive them to job interviews. I can stretch unexpected financial bonuses into blessings for someone else. Maybe we can even cut out a few luxuries we take for granted, just so we have a little extra to give away.

I don't think we all have to rush to a third-world country and give away all our money to the poor. But we all should give. Be wise and not foolish. Put Christ first. But be generous and give. Care. Love. What great benefit it will bring — not just to people watching us, but also to our own souls — to do good in this way.

People in need are not just "the poor" to me these days. May I continue to see them as what they truly are — God's unique creations, with individual stories and destinies that are unfolding every day.

A villager washed her clothes as usual in a river that is home to crocodiles, herons, and piranhas.

This boy fervently wanted Tom to go for a ride in his canoe. However, there was a large split in the center of the boat and crocodilian eyes poking up through the plant life in the river. Tom declined.

ONE DROP

by Janine

A drop — just a drop —
A silvery bead of salt water
in a tumbling sea

A drop cannot slow
or shift the direction of
a mighty ocean.

A drop cannot turn,
in gallons of waves swelling,
the taste of the brine.

But God speaks to me.
Within my heart, a pulse beats,
"A drop. Just a drop."

My face falls, head low.
Am I that tiny?
Insignificant?

196

But God is not done.
"Child, not a drop of water,
But a drop of light."

And He lifts my head.
And shows me the night sky with
Bright pinpoints of fire.

One drop is enough.
For the smallest candle's tip
can transform darkness.

CHAPTER SIXTEEN

PROMISE: WHISPERS FROM OUR HEAVENLY FATHER

By Janine

L EAVING BOLIVIA WAS HARD FOR all four of us. My husband was leaving his dream job — one that combined mechanics, aviation, and helping people in need. I was leaving behind hundreds of children that I cared about deeply and might never see again. My sons were leaving the city they had called home for most of their lives. We all left behind friends who felt like family, a church we loved, and a ministry that we had invested in for nineteen years. Seven of those years were spent on Bolivian soil.

We were all sad and perhaps a bit bewildered as God called us to a new place. Although Tom and I knew for certain we were to move our little family back to our birth country, we did not know what lied ahead. We had a lot of questions. Our younger son, though, who was twelve years old at the time, wasn't just sad and bewildered.

He was angry.

He didn't want to go back to the United States. He wanted to stay right where he was. He pleaded, bargained, and yelled. His anger was understandable. He was being asked to leave his home. Who wouldn't be upset about that? But Tom and I knew that we were meant to leave just as strongly as we had known we were to come years before. We trusted God and were going to obey wherever He led, knowing that He would do what was best in our lives. Philip was wrestling with that.

Steve Saint, whose life literally is material for a movie script, once wrote this message to our son: "God writes beautiful stories. Let Him write yours." I share this part of Philip's story, with his permission, because it is a mighty reminder of how God cared for us the whole way through our South American journey — even to the teary morning at the airport on our last day there. God is so personal and loving. He had a plan even when we didn't understand and couldn't yet see the final chapters.

It was about one week until departure day. We ate out more often as boxes were packed and the refrigerator and cabinets were emptied. Piles of our possessions stood in our way while we dug to the bottoms of cupboards and closets, deciding what to keep, what to sell, what to store, what to bring, what to give away, what to throw out.

Hours were in short supply, and I began condensing errands to save time. I shopped closer to the house and settled on things that weren't exactly what I wanted, so I could just hurry and get the job done. One day, instead of going to the open-air market for decent, reasonably priced lemons and then continuing on to the air-conditioned grocery store where meat and milk were kept in coolers, I just bought everything at the store. My lemons were not handed to me by a farmer, but bagged and stickered like they often are in US supermarkets.

After I got home, Philip looked at what I bought and got upset. He wanted to know why I had chosen *those* lemons with *that* sticker. I didn't know what he was talking about. I started to say something about not having enough time for two stores today and took the lemons from him. Then, I saw — and smiled. I didn't think much of it when I bought them, but the lemons were labeled with a name — which happened to be the name of the town we were moving to in North America. What are the odds of that?

I told Philip that it wasn't intentional, but it was kind of a cool coincidence, wasn't it? He stormed away.

A few days later, about two-thirds of the house had been

packed. Our furniture was disappearing, a piece or two at a time. Bit by bit, we were piling all of our smaller boxes into the tiniest room in the house as we emptied and cleaned the other rooms.

Peter's bedroom was bare, but Philip was struggling to finish cleaning out his. So that morning, I decided to give him a hand. He had just woken up, and I sat cross-legged on the tile floor, starting to sort and drag stray bits from behind and beneath the furniture. He came and sat beside me.

"Mom?" he said softly. "Do you know Isaiah 55:8?"

"No," I answered, "but I can find it for you." I reached for a Bible on his bookshelf. "Why do you ask?"

Still groggy, he mumbled that he had heard someone say that reference to him in his dream while he slept.

I opened the Bible to the writings of the prophet Isaiah and read these words from God to my son: "'For my thoughts are not your thoughts, neither are your ways my ways,' declares the Lord. 'As the heavens are higher than the earth, so are my ways higher than your ways and my thoughts than your thoughts'" (Isaiah 55:8-9 NIV).

Philip and I sat in amazed silence, just looking at each other. The Bible contains more than 30,000 verses. But Isaiah 55:8? Philip picked that one, in a sleep-induced daze, by accident? A random chance? I can't believe that. I believe God was speaking.

Friends came over to the house to help us move. We were working hard to finish. It was less than forty-eight hours until we would be airborne, headed to our new chapter of life in the United States. Philip's room was coming along, slowly but surely. My office—buried in books and papers for most of my stay in Bolivia—was starting to clear. Loose ends at our jobs were being tied up, and difficult goodbyes were being said.

We took our helpful friends to lunch at the same shopping center where I had bought the lemons. We split up in search of pizza, chicken, burgers, and such, and Philip and I ended up in a buffet line. We neared the counter and Philip's temper flared again. "Mom! Really?"

I looked where he pointed and laughed. How could I not?

A sticker on this South American cash register proclaimed the acronym for the school he was transferring to 6,600 miles away.

I thought of the words of a schoolmate in Costa Rica — a man whose name I don't even remember now. He once said that sometimes God whispers reminders of His presence and love for us when He knows we need it. Philip was getting whispers — the lemons, the Bible verse, the sticker on the cash register.

But God wasn't done yet.

Philip and I got our food and sat down. The boys were mostly quiet as Tom and I talked with the other couple about things going on in their lives. Toward the end of our meal, a large, elderly woman we didn't know shuffled over to join us.

This was not a quiet restaurant, and our tables weren't bumped together back-to-back on a carpeted floor. It was a bustling, noisy food court at lunch hour. There were maybe a hundred people eating and working around the little square tables where we sat. Shoppers wove their way in and out of the grocery store entrance. So when this stranger slowly came to stand beside us and began speaking, it was a bit of a spectacle.

After greeting us, she focused her attention on our younger son. "God gave me a message for you," she told him.

I looked at Philip and wondered if his heart was pounding like mine. This wasn't a common, everyday experience. Our friends were new to the area. I wondered what they were thinking. Across the room, I saw big men — laborers, judging by their appearance — shift their gaze from their plates of food to watch. It was a bit awkward, to put it mildly.

"You must keep your eyes on Jesus," the woman was saying. "Put Him first. Listen to your parents. Do good in school."

Her counsel lasted for about five minutes, as she continued to tell him to stay focused on God's best for him, to do what God wanted him to do in life, and not to get entangled by girls who were trouble and toxic.

We were stunned by this unprecedented moment. We had lived in Bolivia for nearly a decade. Strangers had approached in the past to talk about politics, religion, travel, finances, our height, weight, hair—many things. But a message directly from God? Never in all that time had we been spoken to quite like this. Her list of instructions was like one that we ourselves would have given our son as he started a new school, grade, and community — encouraging him to keep his focus where it should be. But we had never told this woman a thing about our lives, including what an enormous turn Philip's life was making that week, what a huge time of transition it was for both of our sons.

We thanked her, and Philip hugged her. In parting, she asked if she could know his name, so that she could continue to pray for him. He told her the Spanish equivalent, Felipe. When she heard it, she smiled gently.

"I'll remember that name," she said. "That's my grandson's name."

We went home and returned to the task of cleaning Philip's room. We talked about how God doesn't usually work quite like that, although He certainly can. We talked about how God loved Philip and knew he needed some extra assurances during such a difficult time of parting from a place and people that he loved. Tom, Peter, and I were wondering and hurting, too, make no mistake. But we were already relying on our Savior to be there for us. Philip needed a little extra encouragement to prepare him for this move. So God, in His love and wisdom, chose not to force him to walk in the blind faith which is often good for us—but to reveal whispers of His love, day after day. He sent reminders that He was leading and walking with us.

Later that day, a friend came to say goodbye. He was a man who had worked side by side with us over the course of many years. He was usually a quiet person, but this time he had some things to say. Unaware of our lunchtime adventure, he repeated nearly word-for-word what the elderly woman had said to Philip.

We hardly knew what to do next. The man walked back out of the door, and Philip turned to me with wide, questioning eyes.

"I know!" I replied to his unspoken statement.

"Could I... Should I... ?"

"Tell him!"

Philip raced out to the car that was about to leave and told the man what the guest to our lunch table had said to him. The man cried. I cried. We hugged goodbye. What a gift we had all been given.

At the time of this writing, we have been stateside for nearly four years. There have been many wonderful days and moments. We have new jobs, new ministries, and some new friends, and we are so grateful. Yet there have been difficult moments, too. In those times of homesickness and heartache, what a profound joy and blessing it has been to look back and see metaphorical piles of rocks, symbols of God's care for us all along the way.

Psalm 139, a well-known passage of scripture written by the poet-King David, says that God knew each of us before we were even born, that He knit us together in our mother's womb.

I love this thought. But there is another verse, this one penned by the prophet Isaiah, which also means a great deal to me, especially as I get older. It works like a complimentary bookend for Psalm 139. It says, "Even to your old age and gray hairs I am He, I am He who will sustain you. I have made you and I will carry you; I will sustain you and I will rescue you" (Isa. 46:4 NIV).

From birth to death, beginning to end, and everywhere in between, our God is faithful. So, day after precious day, by His grace and mercy, we keep stacking up stones.

ACKNOWLEDGMENTS

Tom and Janine would like to thank:

Peter and Philip—Thanks for giving us time and encouragement to write these pieces of our story. You are awesome men and we love you more than words can say! May you always, to the cores of your beings, be aware of God's INFINITE faithfulness.

Audrey, a.k.a. Mom—Thanks for pouring so much time and emotion into this. You are an amazing editor and working with you has been a gift. In this, and so many other journeys, thank you for your encouragement and prayers! We love you!

George, a.k.a. Dad—Thanks for your enthusiasm, faithful reading and discussions of our manuscript. It has been a pleasure to share this project with you and to share your book projects, as well! Thank you for loving, supporting and cheering us on for so many years. We love you!

Terry and Marlene, a.k.a. Dad and Mom—Thank you for coming to Bolivia often to visit, encourage, and work beside us, and for helping others develop a deeper love for the Bolivian people. You have made a difference in so many lives in South and North America. Your giving and loving example is priceless to us. We love you!

Debbie Loudermilk—We are so glad to count you as a friend. We are also deeply grateful for your generosity in reading and proofreading our manuscript so carefully. You made our book much better and even taught us more about English along the way... bonus! :) Thank you, thank you, thank you! We love you!

Our Editor, Lois Flowers — You went above and beyond to see this project through and we are grateful to have had your help and insights to make this book more than we could have on our own. Thank you! http://www.loisflowers.com/

Glendon Haddix of Streetlight Graphics — Thank you for your beautiful design work that helped bring our hopes to reality. We are blessed and grateful. http://www.streetlightgraphics.com/

Our supporting churches — Six California churches lovingly, faithfully supported us in our missionary journey with prayer, finances and even some manpower when we needed it. Thank you, Arcata First Baptist Church; Eureka First Baptist Church; Grace Fellowship Church of Amador County; Gualala Baptist Church; Redwood Chapel of Castro Valley and Valley Community Church of Pleasanton. May God bless you for your service to Him.

La Iglesia Vida Eterna — We worked with many churches in South America, but this one was our "home-away-from-home." Gracias a nuestros hermanos de la Iglesia Vida Eterna. Los amamos por siempre en el amor de Dios. Somos mas que compañeros. Somos familia. Gracias por su apoyo, amistad, oraciones y amor. Que Dios los bendiga siempre. Y que siempre anden con El.

Janine would also like to thank:

So many people whose motivating comments helped propel us forward in this project — Thank you for your nudges, shoves, cheers, enthusiasm and especially your prayers. Every kind word touched my heart!

My sweet husband, Tom — What a gift to be able to write a book and live life with such a talented, amazing man! Thanks for walking with me through all these stories and constantly pointing my eyes to our Jesus. ¡Te amo por siempre!

Would you like to share Stacking Stones with your book club, missions work team or Sunday School class?

Write us at jcthrossel@gmail.com or visit www.janinethrossel.com for information about how you can get group discounts and a free Discussion Guide!

Above: Philip with a monkey at a Bolivian animal rescue shelter.

Below: Peter in a Cessna 206 airplane, en route to a rural community.

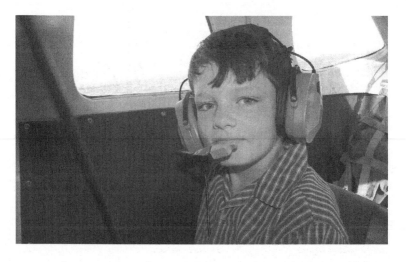

Above: A view that was quite familiar to our family – out the window of a Cessna 206.

Below: This momma and chicks huddled in a rainstorm, reminding us of God's promises that he can gather and shelter us in the storms of life. "He shall cover you with his feathers, and under his wings you shall take refuge." – Psalm 91:4a, NKJV.

Above: Our sons went nearly everywhere with us, so they often had to entertain themselves during long flights, road trips, hospital waits, meetings and queues. They used their incredible creativity to invent stories, songs, artwork, imaginary video games and board games like this one, created somewhere between California and Bolivia.

Below: Highland women dancing in a parade. Their elaborate costumes and gold jewelry are so valuable that bodyguards often accompany them along the parade route.